MEN'S PIE MANUAL

AUTHOR'S ACKNOWLEDGMENTS
Thanks first and foremost to my wife, Kate, and my daughter, Matilda, for being such good pie testers. Thanks to Louise McIntyre and all the team at Haynes for doing such a great job on the book. My thanks to Antony Topping and Claudia Young, my agents at Greene and Heaton. Thanks to Stefan Johnson for the excellent photography that heads up each chapter and the cover. My thanks also to the chefs and food writers who contributed recipes and image. Finally, thanks to you, the reader, for buying this book. You're going to buy it aren't you? Course you are... it's about pies!

First published October 2014

A catalogue record for this book is available from the British Library

ISBN 978 0 85733 287 5

Library of Congress catalog card no. 2014930862

Haynes Publishing,
Sparkford, Yeovil, Somerset BA22 7JJ, UK
Tel: +44 (0) 1963 442030
Fax: +44 (0) 1963 440001
E-mail: sales@haynes.co.uk
Website: www.haynes.co.uk

Haynes North America, Inc.,
861 Lawrence Drive, Newbury Park,
California 91320, USA

Printed in the USA by Odcombe Press LP,
1299 Bridgestone Parkway, La Vergne, TN 37086

Author	Andrew Webb
Project manager	Louise McIntyre
Designer	James Robertson
Copy editor	Ian Heath
Principal photography	Stefan Johnson
General photography	Andrew Webb
	Shutterstock
Food stylist for cover	Katie Marshall

MEN'S PIE MANUAL

The complete guide to making and baking the perfect pie

Andrew Webb

Contents

INTRODUCTION

Gentleman, we apparently live in a culinary 'have it all' age: there is practically nothing you cannot buy ready-made from one of the chiller cabinets of Britain's many shops. And that includes pies, from 'four for a £1' mystery meat offerings to celebrity chef-endorsed fancy ones.

So why make your own? Well, food scares have made many a man look anew at where the food on his table comes from; you see, if you make it, you know *exactly* what's in it. But more than that, to make a pie for someone is to give them the gift of time itself. What you're really doing is saying 'Look, I made you a stew, then I let it *go cold* and *then* I put it in some pastry I've made to make it taste even better!'

Pies, like cakes, are made for sharing, for conviviality and company. They're something communal, and recall a time when meals where more social occasions. And they're fun, and pretty much everyone likes pie, right? Because when you bring a big golden pie to the table and gently break into that flaky, crumbly pastry, or pop a steamed pudding and let the filling slowly tumble out, anyone who isn't impressed isn't worthy of your efforts or worthy of space at your table – fetch their coat.

Of course, with a bit of planning you can make things a bit easier for yourself; you see, pies are the best use of any leftovers known to man. Had a roast chicken on Sunday? Put all the leftover meat and veg in a pie (page 129). Done a bit of blackberrying with the kids or got some fruit on the turn in the fruit bowl? Then make a fruity pie (page 150). Seen a bargain at the butchers or greengrocers or supermarket? The rule is simple: bulk buy, and think pie. In fact you've probably got enough bits in your fridge, cupboard and freezer to rustle up a pie right now. It's that easy.

SO WHAT'S A PIE?

There is a trinity of magical things that make the perfect pie. Firstly there's the filling – chunks of meat, vegetables, fish or fruit; it's this that give the pie texture and taste, as well as its name. Then there's the sauce in which the filling is suspended: too thick, and your pie will be dry; too thin, and your pie will be watery and will leak. Finally,

there's the pastry, which provides structure and the casing, as well as soaking up the sauce. When these three things are done right, in the right proportions, a pie achieves something much greater than the sum of its parts.

Andrew Webb
May, 2014

CHAPTER 1
TOOLS OF THE TRADE

Making pies and puddings doesn't require anything that you can't find in a normal kitchenware shop, online, or even in a well-stocked department store; but it's worth getting the right equipment for the job, and taking good care of it.

Add equipment piece by piece as you need it, rather than buying loads of stuff in one go. That way, you'll have time to become familiar with it. National treasure Mary Berry once told me she still bakes in the tins she got as a wedding present 'many years ago', admitting she'd be totally stumped if she had to use, say, a brand new silicone casing to make a pie or a cake. Familiarity breeds content.

A word about costs. It's really worth buying the best you can afford for some key everyday items such as knives, as well as tins which will hold all your hard work while it cooks. A certain popular Swedish store may sell four knives for just over a tenner, but in my experience they'll not last long. Like so many things in a chap's life – watches, aftershave, suits – it's better to buy from a firm that specialises in each item. Other items that don't get so much use and abuse can be from more budget lines. Another way to save money (so you can invest it in other better quality stuff) is to wait until the January or summer sales, where you can often pick up bargains as stores clear out old – but perfectly good – stock.

Once you're under way buying kit can get slightly addictive: I'm a total sucker for a beautifully laid-out kitchenware shop staffed by a smiley sales lady gifted in the arts of shopping seduction and up-selling. That tingling sensation you feel in your pocket, gentlemen, is your credit card melting, so stay focused and try to resist the garlic peeling gadget, the tall asparagus saucepan or whatever, as they'll barely see the light of day.

Knives, chopping boards, tongs, spatulas

KNIVES

Everything starts with a knife, and I cannot stress the importance of buying a really good one. Your knife is your kitchen Excalibur, your Glamdring, your Sword of Omens. You're nothing without it – a king without a sword, a kitchen without a king! – so take good care of it.

It should be the first thing you wash up (don't put it in the dishwasher), dry up, and put back in its box. Yes that's right. Buy a knife that comes in a box and keep it there. The quickest way to ruin a knife is to leave it rattling around at the bottom of a sink full of dirty dishes or loose in a cutlery drawer. It'll just get damaged and blunt.

A good knife should feel weighty and balanced in the hand. When you first get it home get some carrots and spend some time test-driving it, so that you're comfortable and familiar with it for the real thing.

I favour Zwilling/Henckels knives, a company that's been making knives in Germany since the 1730s. Hammer Stahl is a new company that makes some lovely knives too. Other people favour Global knives from Japan, while Heston Blumenthal endorses Tojiro. Indeed, many Western knife-makers are producing Japanese-style blades now, which tend to be more slender. 'Santoku'-style knives are quite popular; this 'all-rounder' variety of knife comes from Japan and its name means 'three virtues', referring to chopping, slicing and mincing. They often have little scalloped holes running along the length of the blade, the benefit being that food is less inclined to stick to the blade when cut. The downside is that due to the blade shape they're not as 'rockable' (a fast chopping motion where you hold down the tip of the knife with the palm of your other hand) as Western-style knives. Try a few out in the store before you buy.

Much like the top-flight Premiership football teams, there's probably very little difference between quality knife producers. There is, however, a world of difference between them and the cheap, mass-produced knives from the 'third division' manufacturers that you'll find in a supermarket. Be careful if you see a Sabatier knife for a bargain price, as many knife-makers in France use that name; some are excellent, but many others are cheaper mass-market products.

As well as a 6in–8in (15–20cm) chef's or cook's knife, you'll also need a vegetable knife. Smaller, with typically a 2.5in (6cm) blade, these little knives are for more delicate vegetable work, as well as trimming pastry. The same care rules apply, however.

With these two knives you can pretty much do everything you'll need to do in a kitchen. Having said all of this, I do know of one well-established chef who does everything in his kitchen with an old bread knife, but he's the exception that proves the rule! A bread knife does come in handy when portioning pies, however: to cut through cold, harder pies like pork pies or gala pie a sawing motion

with a bread knife is far more effective than applying pressure with a chef's knife.

STEELS AND STONES

A steel is a round bar with tiny grooves on it that sharpens a knife by repeatedly running it up and down the blade at the correct angle. To be honest, unless you're a chef and use one every day they're probably not worth the money. You'll do far better to invest in a whetstone and sharpen your knives once every few months on that. It doesn't look as showy and cheffy as using a steel, but you'll not have someone's eye out or loose a thumb, and it'll actually get your knives sharper.

CHOPPING BOARDS

The person responsible for inventing the glass chopping board probably did so after his chocolate fireguard and inflatable dartboard

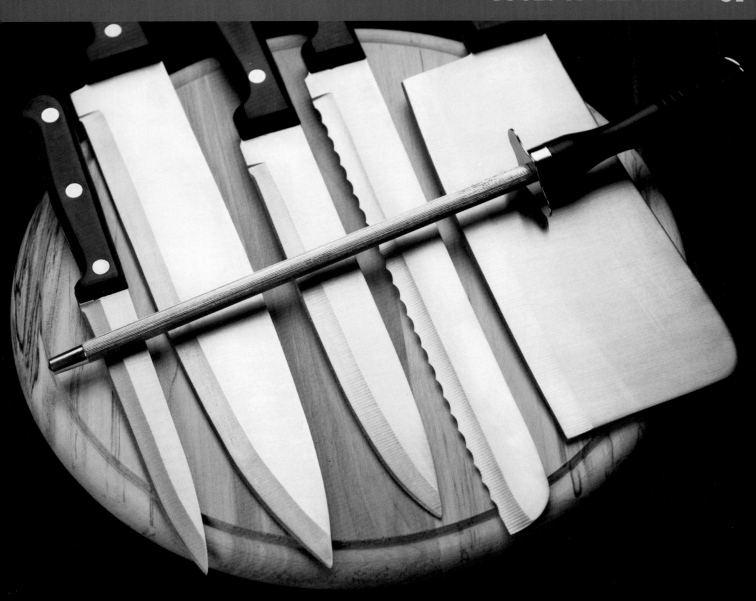

ideas were rejected. Never buy one. Buy two big wooden chopping boards, one for raw meat and one for cooked items and other work. Like knives, wooden chopping boards are no friend of dishwashers, which cause the wood to warp, so it's out with the washing-up liquid and hot tap to keep these clean.

I find plastic boards don't come big enough for domestic use. Having one or two about to chop herbs on is fine, but for real kitchen work like butchery you need a big, thick, wooden board that can take a pounding.

A piece of damp kitchen roll, or better still, a J-cloth, placed underneath whichever board you use will keep it from moving about.

KITCHEN TONGS

With the rise of TV chefs in the 1990s viewers didn't want to see chefs handling items with their bare hands (which is what happens in a real kitchen most of the time, let me assure you), so we started to see tongs being used a lot more.

Tongs make moving hot things around pans a doddle for those of us without asbestos fingers. Ideally you want two pairs, a metal pair for hard, hot work, and a plastic or rubbery-tipped pair that you can use on non-stick pans without scratching them.

SPATULAS AND SPOONS

A spatula is a handy piece of kit for mixing thick sauces, as well as for spreading items such as fried onions or mushrooms. Half a dozen wooden spoons are essential for pie-making. Try to get ones with long handles and a big 'spoon' end. Again, being wood they're no friends of prolonged water exposure.

Saucepans and frying pans

Now, you've probably got some pots and pans in your kitchen already, but below is a list of things that I've found invaluable, so plug any gaps in your pan collection. Your pans are going to take a lot of abuse over the course of your pie-making as well as other cooking, so get good ones. Plastic handles don't get as hot as metal ones, obviously, but they can end up coming loose.

Saucepans can be either ordinary or non-stick, but I personally think you only need non-stick for a frying or sautéing pan. Generally non-stick pans are more delicate, and eventually – even if you never put a metal utensil near it – the non-stick coating does wear out. There's also been some health and environmental concerns around non-stick.

Whenever cooking with pans, always use a lid. Things will cook quicker, water will boil faster, and you'll save energy.

MILK PAN

A small pan that's great for making a quick roux (see page 52) or other sauce. Has a spout on each side too, for easier pouring. You only need one of these.

MEDIUM SAUCEPAN

A mid-sized all-rounder pan. Try to find one with high sides – this helps keep things in if you're mashing or doing some frantic stirring. Best to have at least two or three of these in the kitchen.

LARGE SAUCEPAN

May still have a handle like its medium brother, but is a better pan for boiling bigger things like potatoes. High sides are again important if you're using this pan to steam a pudding.

CASSEROLE

A big pan, with two side handles, often made from cast iron, so heavy. Why do many recipes start 'in a heavy-bottomed casserole'? I've yet to see a 'light-bottomed casserole', but they must exist. I've a battered old *Le Creuset* one I got in a sale. In my experience, though, other cast iron enamelled brands are just as good. Enamelled pans are as happy in the oven as on the stove, and these types of pan really come into their own for potato-topped dishes, like shepherd's pie (page 116) or fish pie (page 104). Also, they're acceptable to send to table, unlike a pan with a long single handle; not sure why that is.

STOCKPOT

The bigger the better. I use a huge one that goes by the nickname 'Big Bertha', in which I can easily poach a whole chicken. Stock pans are also good if you're cooking in bulk and freezing, and I once made a chilli for 20 in Bertha.

FRYING PANS

Again, if you've got the space a range of sizes helps. Little 6in (15cm) ones are great for quickly browning small amounts of meat, while having a large non-stick high-sided sautéing pan with a glass lid is great for one-pot super-dishes, as well as sealing meat in larger amounts. I also have a third frying pan I use only for fish.

Other stove-top things

STEAMERS
Steamers – perforated containers that sit on top of saucepans – are good for cooking vegetables such as broccoli and other greens that you then might use in a pie. By steaming them to al dente rather than boiling, they keep their shape and structure rather than turning to mush.

GRIDDLE PANS
Not that relevant to pie-making, but handy to have if you want to get that charred stripe on vegetables and meat.

TINY PANS
Many gastro pubs send side-orders to table in little copper pans. Take a leaf out of their book and make individual mini pies (see page 82) – just don't call them 'canapies'.

Pastry brush, crimpers, pastry cutters, rolling pins

So far the kit we've looked at is good for all cookery, but now we're in the realm of the pie-maker and baker – these tools make working with your pastry easier, and the end result look more professional.

PASTRY BRUSH

Pretty much essential for egg washing your pies, which gives them that lovely golden shine. Silicone ones are now available, the benefit being they won't leave the odd hair in your cooking like the old wooden ones can. I have, on occasion, when 'playing an away match' in a strange kitchen, resorted to using a clean child's paintbrush. And on one memorable occasion I dabbed a pie with a piece of kitchen roll soaked in egg wash, which I can confirm doesn't work nearly as well.

ROLLING PIN

The cooking cudgel, rolling pins are the baseball bats of the kitchen. The cheapest of the cheap are wooden with no moving parts. Plastic ones are available too. Other designs have a central drum that revolves round two handles, and if you're really serious you might consider a marble or ceramic one. These, unlike wood, stay colder, and heat is the enemy of all pastry work. Whichever you use, remember to dust it with a little flour before you start rolling. Finally, if you're ever somewhere without your kit you could be like my Granny, who used an old milk bottle. Putting it in the fridge first is even better.

simply by shaking, others have a spring-loaded trigger, or you can make one from an old jam jar by simply punching a few holes in the lid with a knife or skewer. They're also handy for dusting sugar on to things.

RULERS AND GUIDES

Here's a tip I adapted from my ceramics teacher at art school. If you're after a consistent thickness to your pastry and you've an ounce of DIY ability, make yourself two rolling guide sticks. These need to be to flat, wide batons of wood, about the thickness of two pound coins on top of each other. Placing these guides either side of your pasty and your rolling pin on top of them as you roll ensures an even depth to your pastry. You might be able to buy these, but they're dead easy to make from any off-cut strip of wood.

FLOUR DUSTER

You'll dust your bench and surface regularly when making pies, so a flour duster makes that process a lot easier. Some work

Mixing bowls and food processors

A good large mixing bowl has a host of uses, aside from just making your pastry in it. They're also great for bashing meat into a marinade, and even proving dough. I'd recommend a decent ceramic one for show, and a couple of cheaper plastic versions to bring up the rear. Pound shops are excellent places to pick up the latter.

FOOD PROCESSORS AND MIXERS

Now, you don't *need* either of these to make a pie, but they do make life in the kitchen easier. For those of you without a dishwasher, however, there's often a trade-off in time and washing-up. Food processors can make pastry in a fraction of the time you can with your hands, and you don't end up with dough-clagged fingers. Also, despite the speed and friction, pastry made in a food processor will be cooler than that made with your hands.

They're also great for things like dicing vegetables, slicing potatoes, blitzing things, making mayonnaise, and a host of other tasks. But I'm going to strike a note here for taking things slow, and say that there's something of 'the journey' – if you've got the time – about chopping an onion or making pastry by hand, that adds to the charm of making a proper pie.

Of course, buying a food processor or mixer means you can spend ages poring over online reviews and agonising over things in department store showrooms. Man does not buy any kit on impulse, but only after slow, methodical digestion of the facts. By which time a new model is out and the process starts again.

Baking beads and baking paper

BAKING BEADS

These are little balls of clay that sit on top of your baking parchment to weigh it down. Of course, you can use large dried beans, which work just as well, or even rice or lentils. Just make sure your paper is secure, as the fan in the oven blew mine aside once, and I was left picking dry lentils out of soggy pastry with a pair of tweezers.

BAKING PARCHMENT

Sounds like something the Egyptians would have used, but parchment, like foolscap, is just an olde worlde word for paper. In fact baking parchment is a rather modern product. The paper is coated with silicone, which makes it totally non-stick. It's normally white, rather than brown like greaseproof. They *say* it removes the need for greasing cake tins, but if I were you I'd butter 'em just to make sure.

GREASEPROOF PAPER

Similar to baking parchment, but often brown rather than white. To be honest I use this and baking parchment interchangeably. Greaseproof paper is also useful for making a 'cartouche' – essentially a paper lid that you put over stews and casseroles to stop a dark skin forming on top, while still allowing the stew to reduce while in the oven. Just remember to make one *before* you start cooking! If your casserole pan has fairly straight sides sit it on the paper, draw round it with a pencil and cut out the resulting circle shape.

CLING FILM

You can even blind-bake with cling film in the oven – I know, mad eh? – yet I've seen it done. Your oven can't be too hot, and you have to layer the cling film to four or five sheets' thickness. You'll still need baking beads. If you do it right, the cling film will contract slightly as it heats up. A quick search online reveals many people coming a cropper trying this, so it's perhaps best done when you're feeling up for a challenge, of if you've just run out of other kinds of baking paper.

PRICK WITH A FORK

There are plenty of people who just prick the whole base all over with a fork. All paper and beads do is keep the bottom of your pie or flan flat and stop it from browning too much. It all depends on what your filling is, and how wet it is. A rule of thumb is: the wetter and heavier the filling, the more you want to blind-bake the base.

Correct oven and hob use

Go into your kitchen and take a look at your oven in the cold light of day. Could it, perhaps, do with a clean? Has the bulb gone? Give it a bit of a service. Because it's in here that your pie efforts will literally rise or fall. Ovens are a once-a-decade purchase, if that – indeed, you're probably more likely to experience a 'new' oven by moving house than you are by buying a new one.

OVEN THERMOMETER

See that small knob on your oven the size of your thumb? Turning that changes your oven from room temperature to around 230°C over just three-quarters of a turn. This makes most ovens very inaccurate at precise temperature measurement. It's far better to spend a few pounds on an oven thermometer that'll tell you exactly how hot it is inside your oven. And if you've got a digital oven fan, you're still beholden to where the thermostat is situated, which is normally towards the back. Point is, knowing what's going on where the action is is important. So is being able to see inside.

THE HOB

You've probably got a big burner, two medium ones and a small one. Needless to say, the big one heats things faster, so think stir fries and bringing things to the boil quickly, as well as getting a pan super hot for char-grilling meat. The medium ones are all-rounders, and the small one is best used for milk pans and making coffee. Remember, after water comes to the boil it can't really get any hotter, so you're just wasting energy keeping it at full whack. Better to turn it down or move to a smaller burner.

HEAT LEVELS FOR LIQUIDS

- **Rapid boil** – Lots of bubbles, with the heat applied as fast as your stove can manage. Cooks small things very fast; often you bring things to this point and then drop down to...
- **Rolling boil** – Bubbles seemingly turning over themselves. This is much better for poaching bigger things and cooking vegetables.
- **Simmer** – Best applied to non-water-based liquids. Simmering slowly reduces a liquid by volume by evaporating the water element, leaving a concentrated flavour.
- **Ticking over** – Finally there's what I call 'barely ticking over': this is used for very long and slow poaching, and for making stocks. It's as low a heat as your cooker can do, and is best used on large pots of liquid. You should be able to dip your finger quickly in liquids at this temperature without resulting in a trip to casualty, though I should point out that, should you end up there, don't blame me.

GLOVES

Get yourself a big, thick, pair of oven gloves. I tend to favour two mitts, with a long sleeve, rather than those 'handcuffs' types. It's worth shelling out a few extra quid here, even if you've got asbestos hands. You don't want to drop your efforts because they're too hot.

Oven temperatures

A word about oven temperatures in this book. Nearly everyone these days has a fan-assisted oven measured in degrees Celsius, so all the cooking times are given for that. If you've not got a fan oven, up the temperature by about 20°C; if you've got a gas mark one, there are conversion tables online.

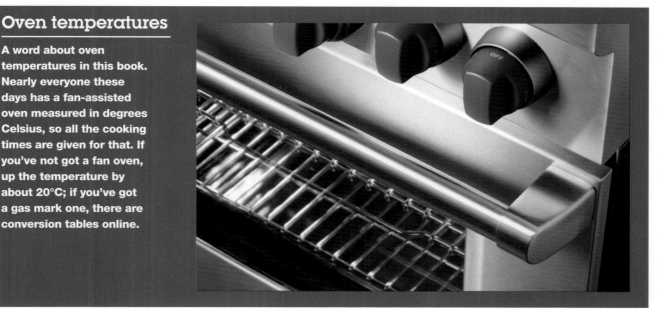

Pie tins and baking sheets

PIE TINS

If you're making a double crust pie, as in a pie that has pastry at the bottom and sides as well as on top, you need to use metal tins – ceramic pie dishes just don't conduct the heat well enough to get the base of your pie crisp, and no one likes a soggy bottom.

Metal pie tins, dishes and plates come in a variety of shapes, depths and sizes. They can be black non-stick ones or enamelled ones. Pie plates are just that, metal plates that give you a shallow pie that's easy to portion into wedges. You can even buy foil pie plates, but I wouldn't recommend it. What you save in pennies you lose in worry about structural integrity. I just don't trust them.

Metal flan dishes have straighter sides than pie plates, but can still be used to make a good pie. Look for one with a rim that's separate to the base plate – this makes getting your pastry creation out a lot easier.

High-sided tins are best used for pork and other 'solid' pies that you would eat cold. These too have a loose base plate, allowing you to get the pie out.

Springform tins are rather rare these days. They're traditionally used for making cold game pies, and have a hinge at one end allowing you to get the pie out. If you find one, buy it, as they do make a fantastic-looking pie.

Keep an eye out in bric-a-brac shops for old pie tins and dishes. You can pick up some real gems, and all they'll need is a bit of elbow grease to get them back into shape.

Finally, you'd be surprised what you can make a pie in – any metal container is fair game, so think small frying pan, loaf tin or tin cup. If you fancy getting a bit silly there are some great novelty cake tins out there you can experiment with. See the upside-down Darth Vader pie on page 179 as an example.

Lakeland do a huge range of easy to use pie tins, some complete with bottom crispers that allow the heat in through little holes, meaning no more soggy bottoms. Check out the suppliers section on page 184 for more information.

BAKING SHEETS

A flat, non-stick baking sheet is essential for crisping up the underside of things like pasties, sausage rolls and Wellingtons – basically anything made without using a tin. You want a range of sizes, from a 'width of your oven' big one to a few smaller ones. I think ones with a very slight lip are better, just in case any of your creations have filling that boils out; then it won't drip all over the bottom of the oven and burn.

Pastry amounts for specific tin sizes

Many of the recipes in this book don't give specific pastry amounts. That's because tins come in all sorts of shapes, depths and sizes, and yours might be totally different to mine. Also, many of the pies can be made as single or double crust, depending on what you prefer. Furthermore you can make a single large one, or portion out the filling to make individual ones.

On top of that, the type of pastry used is sometimes interchangeable too, so if you fancy puff pastry single-crust rather than shortcrust double, you can make that change and adjust cooking times accordingly.

Consequently all these variables make giving specific quantities tricky, so what I've done here is take a selection of popular pie dishes and work out how much pastry each one needs for a double- and single-crust pie.

Lakeland do a range of traditional blue-and-white enamelled bakeware that's great for double- and single-crust pies. As the size increases the tins also get deeper, so you'll need more for the bottom part of a double-crust pie.

- **Small:** 150g for a single crust + 150g for a double crust (total 300g)
- **Medium:** 150g for a single crust + 200g for a double crust (total 350g)
- **Large:** 250g for a single crust + 350g for a double crust (total 600g)
- **Extra-large:** 450g for a single crust + 550g for a double crust (total 1kg)

1kg may seem like a lot, but remember, you'll trim off a fair bit as no pastry rolled ever fits exactly.

There are also round tin pie plates. These tend to be about 9in/24cm across and need about the same-sized pastry for top and bottom, as they're rather shallow.

- 24cm pie plate: 315g for a single crust + 330g for a double crust

Individual round pie tins are the same as their oblong cousins, needing 150g for the top and another 150g for the bottom.

Deeper pie tins are available, some with removable bottom plates. These are still around 20 to 25cm in diameter, but their greater depth means you need 320g for a single crust and 370g for a double crust. Ceramic dishes are only used for single-crust pies.

Ceramic dishes are only used for single-crust pies. The one in the accompanying picture serves four and needs 250g of pastry for a top crust ...

... whereas the oval dish serves one and needs 150g for a single crust.

Of course, much depends on how thick you roll your pastry, and all pastries behave differently. I would advise buying a pack of ready-made puff pastry and a pack of ready-made shortcrust, and rolling each out and cutting to fit your range of tins. Then make a note on the space below:

You could even scratch a number or mark into the base of each tin so that you can identify it. That way you know that 'tin A' serves four, and requires 600g pastry for a double-crust pie. Such information won't make you popular at parties, but it'll ensure people enjoy your cooking, which *will* make you popular.

Round and oval ceramic dishes

Though no good for double-crust pies, ceramic dishes come into their own for single-crusted or potato-topped pies. These dishes can be either round, oval or square. You want something that's about 4cm to 6cm deep – any deeper and you'll have too much filling compared to topping. You also don't want a dish too big in area, as the pastry will sink into the middle, get soggy and won't rise. Buy a selection of dishes of various shapes and sizes and get to know how much topping or pastry each one needs.

Pie funnels

Help is at hand in preventing a soggy middle in large pies in the form of a pie funnel, also known as a 'pie vent' or a 'pie bird'. Today these are often shaped like baby blackbirds, mouth open, presumably after the 'four and twenty' that were baked in a pie. In the past, however, they came in all shapes and sizes. People even collect them. I kid you not – check out http://piebirdsunlimited.com.

HOW TO USE A PIE FUNNEL

You can use a pie funnel in double- and single-crust pies, though more shallow pies made in plate tins won't need one. Place your pie bird in the centre of your dish and spoon your filling around it. To get your lid on, make a cross-shaped slit in middle of the pastry and force it over the head of the pie bird, pulling it tight to the edges. Then slam it in a hot oven asap.

HELP! I'VE NOT GOT A PIE FUNNEL

Fret not, there are a number of things you can do until the postman arrives with the one you've ordered off the Internet. One, make sure your dish and filling are cold. Two, don't fill the dish up too much – two-thirds full is fine. Also, if there's a big chunk in your filling, try and position that in the middle, and smooth down the rest of the filling around it. Finally, stretch your filling over your pie dish as tight as possible – if you've room to put it back in the fridge after rolling it out, even for a few moments, it'll help. You can also make a pie funnel using a tight cone of greaseproof paper. For more on handling pastry see page 24.

Silicone dishes and individual dishes

SILICONE PRODUCTS

The future, some say. Well, not in this house. I've tried a silicone loaf tin, which bulged at the sides, resulting in a wonky bake. I've not tried any other shaped silicone products. The main issues seem to be lack of browning or crisping-up and, bizarrely, some difficulty in getting the finished pie or cake out of the dish.

RAMEKINS

Ramekins are small ceramic bowls with thick, straight sides that can take the heat of an oven with ease. They're great if you're serving individual pies, and because of their small size there's no danger of your pastry top sinking in the middle.

EVERYTHING ELSE

You can use a wide variety of vessels and containers to make pies. See page 82 for my espresso cup pie, which is a great way to start a meal. Frying pans can be used to make a topped pie, as long as they're ovenproof. If you'd like to push the boat out, a traditional fluted game pie mould makes a stunning pie. Indeed, a scouring of junk and antiques shops can often reveal old Victorian pie moulds. I've even seen a mould in the shape of a hedgehog! Victorian jelly moulds might prove interesting as well.

Have a play with the many novelty cake tins that are on the market at the moment. I've used just such a thing for my Darth Vader pie on page 179.

You can even make a pie in a flowerpot – I've seen it done. It goes without saying that it needs to be spotlessly clean before use. If you're not sure, line it with foil. Have a play.

Pudding basins and steamers

PUDDING BASINS

When I was a lad, 'pudding bowl' was a playground haircut insult. Ah, halcyon days. Actual 'pudding bowls' come in two main types, and both need to be used with suet pastry (page 40). Traditional ones are made of ceramic (or sometime glass or metal) and require buttered foil and paper tied with string to form a lid. Reusable plastic ones are much less faff, coming as they do with a plastic lid. Both types come in a range of sizes, from individual to massive four-pint versions that would feed eight or more. Unlike the traditional ceramic ones, plastic ones shouldn't be placed in the oven.

Whichever type you use, it's best to stand your pudding on an upturned saucer to prevent it touching the bottom of the saucepan, fill the pan three-quarters full and then keep an eagle eye on it, as you should never let it boil dry but should keep topping up the water during the cooking process. Remember, you're not boiling it, you're steaming it.

If you fancy some spuds with your pud, you can chuck a few in for the last hour of the cooking time. You could even steam some vegetables on top. How's that for a one-pot supper?

To my mind, there's something wonderful about the warm, damp fug and condensation-covered windows created when making a steamed pudding.

CHAPTER 2

MAKING PASTRY

Of the three things that make a pie – pastry, sauce and filling – pastry is perhaps the most important. It's the container for all your efforts, and also the first thing people see when you serve them. As well as providing structure and form, it also adds a contrast in texture and taste. In times past pastry was much thicker and harder than today, but then it wasn't eaten. Instead it was used more like we use Tupperware, to protect the filling.

Nowadays, of course, pastry is part of the pie-eating process, and best when soaked in the fruity or meaty juices. There are many excellent ready-made pastries available – look out for 'all butter' ones, as these will be good quality and behave like homemade pastry. But do have a go at making your own, it's not that hard. It's also loads cheaper, and you'll have the smug satisfaction of knowing you made every bit of your pie by hand; remember, you're a craftsman, a carpenter of food. There is pride and honour to be had in saying 'I made that'.

There are as many recipes and methods for making pastry on the Internet as there are pictures of cute cats. I've tried most of them so you don't have to. What follows are recipes that work for me. The right amount of both fat and flour is the key to good pastry; sugar comes into play for sweet pies, while a pinch of salt does for savoury (don't omit the salt in sweet pastry either – it gives a nice flavour edge). The final ingredient is water. Time and temperature are the only other things that are needed. Pastry needs time to rest and set – whatever you do, don't rush it.

Tips, cold hands, resting, blind baking

TEMPERATURE

According to the old wives' tale 'cold hands and warm heart' make the pastry, and generally speaking the more you handle, prod, finger and move pastry, the more it gets annoyed and deteriorates. Treat it gently at all times, and it will repay you. The exception is hot water crust (page 38), which, as one female pie-maker put it to me, 'is less "mimsy" than other pastries and needs to be treated firmly'.

MIXING PASTRY

How you choose to combine your fat, flour and liquid is very important. These are the main methods:

Fingertips

Using your fingertips is by far the simplest way to mix pastry, and given that you probably already own a full set they're also the cheapest. Mixing with your fingers allows you to judge the texture of your pastry as it's coming together. If it feels too wet you can add a little more flour; too dry and a drop more water is needed.

The downside with using your fingers is that they're warm, and so if you spend too much time rubbing the fat in you'll start to melt it. This is especially true for blokes like me with big, hot hands. Consequently you have to work quickly.

When using your fingers for rubbing in, always draw the flour and fat up out of the bowl to rub it, letting it fall back as it passes through your fingers.

A food processor

Food processors make making pastry easy, but you do have to be careful not to overdo it. The blade will produce some heat as it spins, so take it really slowly in gentle pulses rather than revving it at full whack.

The two knives method

Favoured by my maternal Scottish grandmother, who made pie at least once a week in old enamelled tin dishes, this technique sees you incorporate the fat and flour together with two knives, preferably round-ended butter knives. You make small cutting motions with the blades.

Pastry blender

An easier version of the two knives approach, some people swear by pastry blenders. You use them like a potato masher – they break the fat up into tiny pieces that help produce a perfect, flaky pastry.

RESTING PASTRY

Apart from hot water crust, pastry needs plenty of rest. It likes nothing more than putting its feet up in a nice cool fridge. This allows the gluten in the flour to start to develop, and the fat to firm up again.

Most pastry tips say roll the dough into a ball, then wrap it in cling film and put it in the fridge. However, I prefer to use sandwich bags (they're reusable and sealable) rather than cling film. Also they

have a white space where you can write what's in them as well as the date, handy if you're going to freeze the pastry.

They're also easier to manage, as I don't know about you, but my roll of cling film *always* ends up out of the box and I'm forever picking along its length trying to find the edge. You only wrap it in plastic to stop it drying out.

Secondly consider the shape. If you put a ball of dough in the fridge the outside will get cold but the centre will probably still be warm after 20 minutes, so my advice is to squash the ball flat into a lozenge shape thereby increasing the surface area, which will let the cold penetrate deeper.

If you can rest pastry overnight it'll be even better. Finally,

remember that pastry freezes well, so always make more than you need. Then you'll have some ready to go for a midweek quick pie.

BLIND BAKING

You'll encounter this term throughout this book. It refers to pre-cooking the bottom and sides of a pastry case to ensure a good firm bake and avoid the dreaded soggy and undercooked bottom. Often baking beads and greaseproof paper are used to weigh the pastry down during cooking (see page 16). Whichever method you use, make sure the pastry goes from a cold fridge to a hot waiting oven. It's that rapid temperature change that shocks pastry into action.

How to roll pastry

COOL YOUR BENCH

Professional pastry chefs roll out their dough on a refrigerated block of marble, in a chilled room, at dawn. That's a little too much for the average pie-making chap, so here's the next-best thing.

Fill a baking tray with ice cubes and place it on your work surface about ten minutes before you start working. This will chill it down. When you remove the tray check for any condensation. If there is any, wipe it away with kitchen roll. You want to begin on as cool and dry a surface as possible. Starting mid-morning's fine too.

UNDER PRESSURE

Whatever rolling pin you've chosen (see page 14), how you roll is just as important. Lightly flouring your pin to help stop the pastry sticking to it only works up to a point. It's all about how hard you roll too. You want to apply gentle pressure, firmly, but don't force or chase the dough – you're not driving a steamroller. It's better to roll softer for longer.

ROLL FROM THE MIDDLE OUT

When rolling pastry, particularly shortcrust, start in the middle and roll up (away from you), then return to the middle and roll down (towards you). This will slow the gluten development.

MOVE THE PASTRY NOT YOUR PIN

Don't come at your dough from crazy angles. Move and turn the dough gently, and keep your pin rolling straight ahead.

THE QUARTER-TURN

As you roll you'll end up with two thicker ends. Turning 45° flattens these down and ensures an even spread. Moving the pastry also helps stop it sticking to your work surface.

LINING THE TIN

You need to act swiftly when transferring your pastry to your baking tin. The best way is to gently loop the dough over your rolling pin and unfurl it like a magic carpet on to the waiting tin. You want to get this right first time, chaps, so place your tin over your pastry to see if it's big enough. Measure it, and try and imagine what you're going to do next.

Remember, it's not just the diameter of the tin that's important – the pastry has to come up the sides and over the lip too. So you want it a good 2in to 3in (5cm–8cm) bigger than your tin (depending on the deepness of if).

If you do misjudge it, you've got to work fast to get it rolled back loosely around your pin and try again. If you miss a third time, stop. Roll the pastry back into a ball, put it and the tin in the fridge, read something from another chapter of this book for ten minutes and then have another go.

ROLLING ON THE BASE PLATE

If you're using a large non-stick flan tin with a removable base plate you can also roll out your pastry on top of this – slowly, remember. Then, using a fish slice or a palette knife, lift the base plate and place into the outer ring and just work up the edges. This technique lets you get a very thin, flaky crust over a large area, and reduces the risk of it breaking. You'll still need to do quarter-turns as you roll. Hat tip to my friend Rupes, who first showed me this technique.

CAN'T TOUCH THIS!

The fewer times you handle the pastry the better. Once your pastry is loosely over the tin, you need to work it into the corners. Jabbing at it with a hot pointy finger might poke through the pastry, or rip it, as well as not getting it flush into the tin.

Instead take a lump of offcut or leftover pastry, roll it into a ball with your fingertips and pinch and hold it at one end. You've just made a 'dabber'. Use the round ball end to gently press the pastry into the corner of the tin. The dabber also has another use – it's your canary in the mine. I put mine on a baking tray with my pie. Though it's a different size, it allows me to judge how the pastry's behaving in the oven. If all is well you can even eat it as a cook's perk.

ROLLING BETWEEN THE SHEETS

You can enrich your pastry by adding more fat and reducing the flour, or by adding eggs. However, this makes it a bit tricky to roll out and move about on your bench. One answer is to roll it out between two sheets of greaseproof paper. Remember, keep the pastry cool and the fat solid.

Choosing the right flour

FLOUR POWER

All flours are not equal. I've tried economy ranges, and while they're OK for some things I find they have an oddly 'dull' feel in the mouth. Unlike many things there's not that much difference in price between a supermarket own label or economy range and a premium brand. I rather like Marriage's, based in Essex, though Doves and Shipton Mill are good producers too. The bigger commercial producers are the likes of Homepride, Allisons and McDougalls.

Whatever flour you choose, get to know it, and see how well it works for each recipe. Changing flours can produce different results, as gluten levels can vary a great deal.

WHAT'S IN THOSE LITTLE GRAINS?

Each grain of wheat has three components: the bran, endosperm and germ. Bran is the outer casing. It's sieved out of white flour, but you find it in wholemeal varieties. The endosperm is the white starchy body of the wheat. It's this that makes up the bulk of the flour. Finally the germ is the reproductive centre of the grain, and contains nutrients and vitamins.

PLAIN FLOUR

Plain flour is milled wheat with the bran and germ removed. It's often bleached to give it a whiter appearance. Unbleached versions are available but will be more creamy yellow in colour. All shortcrust pastry uses plain flour.

SELF-RAISING

Self-raising flour is just plain flour with baking powder added. Personally I think it's better to use plain flour and just add your own baking powder. A rule of thumb is four teaspoons of baking powder per 225g of flour. Self-raising is used in suet pastry to give a nice open texture. Self-raising is mainly used for cakes. In the USA self-raising flour also contains added salt.

STRONG FLOUR

Made from hard wheat, this has a higher gluten level and is mainly used to make bread. However, it does have uses in pastry; hot water crust and flaky pastry use strong flour, as well as classic puff. The British climate isn't ideal for growing hard varieties of wheat, so they're often imported from Canada, Europe and the USA.

WHOLEMEAL FLOUR

The whole kit and caboodle, this is flour with everything left in. Consequently wholemeal is incredibly good for you, but does give a more rustic look to pastry. You may need to up the liquid content when using it, as it absorbs more water than white flour.

ORGANIC FLOURS

Many artisan bakers, particularly bread makers, favour organic flour. I have to say I've tried organic and non-organic and found no real difference between them in my kitchen. However, organic flours nearly always tend to be stone-milled rather than roller-milled. This traditional method leaves more of the nutrients intact, so there may be a benefit there. If organic's your thing, use that. If not, don't.

BAKING POWDER

Baking powder is made from a weak alkali and acid that releases carbon dioxide when it comes into contact with liquids, which causes dough to rise. This is why many recipes call for the liquids to be added last. Other leavening agents are cream of tartar and bicarbonate of soda, though they're found more in baking than pie-making.

OTHER FLOURS YOU SHOULD KNOW ABOUT

Rice is a grain just like wheat, and can be milled into a flour. Semolina is a very 'hard' flour produced from durum wheat; it's mainly used to make pasta. Cornflour, made from corn or maize, is used in things like tortillas. None of these flours are any good for making pies in my opinion, but if you're gluten intolerant you can try a blend of some of them – to be honest, I'm no expert on gluten-free. Also rubbish for pie-making are things like rye and spelt flours, though they make lovely bread.

Choosing the right fat and liquids

BUTTER

Good butter has taste and texture – it's not some uniform yellow like Play-Doh, but should smell sweet like a meadow, and feel soft to the touch. Baking is nothing without butter. OK, so you *can* make pastry with olive oil or some such, but that doesn't mean you should.

Always weigh your fat exactly. Too much will make the dough very short, meaning it'll be crumbly and difficult to handle. Too little and your pastry will be tough and dry.

Most recipes call for unsalted butter, but then add a pinch of salt to the pastry anyway. There's a reason for this. Firstly it lets you control the salt level exactly – different manufacturers salt their butter to different levels. On the flipside, salted butter lasts longer in the fridge. Me? I use unsalted, but if salted is all I've got in the house and I need a pie quick, who's to know. There's very little taste difference in my experience.

LARD

Lard gets a bad press. It has none of the rural healthy glow of butter; there are no flowers named after lard, only insults. And yet if you bake one pie made half with lard and half with butter, and another that's all butter, I'll stake my plums that most of you will prefer the taste of the half-and-half one. Why? Well, because lard gives a different texture and taste to butter. They're like a fatty yin and yang – they complement and yet contrast. The best lard is made from the fat surrounding the kidneys of pigs; this doesn't have a 'porky' taste, which makes it ideal for baking.

Lard's fall from grace was brought about principally by health concerns – despite the fact that it has less saturated fat, more unsaturated fat and less cholesterol than an equal amount of butter by weight. Also, many commercial pie-makers avoid lard for cultural reasons. But trust me, it'll make your pastry 'short' and flaky and taste brilliant.

DRIPPING

You can make pastry with beef dripping too. I know this because I once picked up dripping instead of lard by mistake when making a hot water crust pastry, and it still worked.

ICED WATER

When adding water to pastry, always make sure that it's as cold as possible. Let the tap run for a while, or put a small glass at the back of the fridge for 15 minutes before starting.

MILK AND EGGS

Eggs can enrich a dough, as well as add colour. You only need one, mind. Milk is used instead of water in certain pastries, such as cobbler dough. Full fat milk will give you the best results.

LEMON JUICE

Adding a few drops of lemon juice to pastry helps stop the gluten in the flour from becoming overworked. It also adds a little flavour, particularly in sweet pies.

Shortcrust pastry

Rich, crumbly, golden shortcrust pastry is, to my mind, an honest, homely sort of pastry. It doesn't get in the way of the filling, but supports it. It also happens to be the easiest pastry to make and, in my experience, the one that goes wrong the least. I also happen to think it's the tastiest.

INGREDIENTS

- 400g plain flour
- 100g butter
- 100g lard
- Pinch of salt
- A few tablespoons of cold water

It's far better to have pastry left over than to find yourself short. Butter and flour aren't that expensive after all. Any leftovers or offcuts can be frozen or used to make something else.

The rule of thumb for shortcrust is a ratio of around half fat to half flour. Unlike some other pastries, you want your fat at room temperature for shortcrust. This is because it needs to be mixed with the flour quickly, and if it's too cold that'll take longer.

If your bowl and fingers start to glisten, however, you've probably overworked the butter. I'd recommend stopping and putting it back in the fridge to cool things down a bit – you may need to add some more flour. Another danger is overworking the gluten in the flour by too much kneading. This will create a hard, tough pastry rather than one that's light and flaky. Too much water is a bad thing too.

What you're after is a loose relationship between all these ingredients, where they're combined enough to hold together, but can easily yield to the slightest pressure from a fork when cooked. The French call this pastry *pâté brisée*.

I've found that 600g of shortcrust is enough to give you a 'top and bottom' pie crust from a tin around 9in/22cm in diameter.

Sweet shortcrust

Like skinning cats (why would anyone want cat-skin in the first place?), there's also more than one way to make shortcrust pastry. I've been experimenting with the frozen grating method. This sees you put your butter in the freezer, then, when it's well solid, use a cheese grater to grate it into the flour. You can then let it come up to room temperature and rub it in quicker because it's already in smaller pieces. I've had some good results with this method, and no cats were harmed.

If you're making a sweet pie you can add sugar to the pastry mix for a sweeter taste. You only need a small amount, however, just enough to lift it a good distance above the salt. Remember, if you've a sweet filling and sweet custard, a cloyingly sweet pastry isn't going to give you much of a flavour profile.

For the ingredients quoted above you'll need 30g of caster sugar. The sugar will also caramelise and help brown the crust.

1 Sieve the flour into a bowl and add the cut-up butter and lard and a pinch of salt.

2 Rub together quickly. You don't need a uniform texture or to rub away for hours, it should take no more than a few minutes. (What you're doing here is coating the flour with the fat so as to slightly inhibit gluten development, which gives shortcrust its tender flaky texture). You actually want bigger lumps of butter present. These will help make the pastry tender and flaky.

3 Add a tablespoon or two of very cold water and gently combine. If it's looking a little dry, add another.

4 Bring together into a ball, squash it a little, and put in a sandwich bag in the fridge for at least an hour, two if you can spare it. It'll be quite happy in the fridge for 48 hours, however. When you come to need it, just roll out swiftly and transfer to your pie dish.

Classic puff pastry

There are two critical ingredients in classic puff pastry, time and patience. Other than that it's just butter, flour and water. However, practically no-one outside of the world of high-end patisseries makes puff pastry from scratch, and anyone that tells you they regularly do and it's '*so easy*' is a total fibber.

INGREDIENTS

- 150g strong flour
- 150g plain flour
- 140mm cold water
- Pinch of salt
- 250g unsalted butter

It's not that it's particularly hard, it's just very, very time consuming. You've got to have time to make it, rest it, roll it, rest it, roll it, and finally, rest it some more. Only then is it ready to use. Even most chefs don't have time for that, so they buy it in. However, once a year, it's worth having a crack at it, just so you stay 'match fit' and dine out on the 'so easy' line for a bit.

Puff pastry gets its puffed-up appearance by rolling very thin layers of butter between layers of dough. As it cooks in a hot oven, the butter melts, giving off steam and fat which causes the very thin layers of dough to puff up and colour. This gives a light, pleasing crunch in the mouth. The French, who know a thing or two about this, call puff pastry *pâté feuilletée*, which means pastry made leaf-like. Another name for it, and indeed the pudding named after it, is *mille-feuille* meaning a thousand leaves.

METHOD

1 Clear your diary and switch your phone to 'do not disturb' as this is going to take a while.
2 Mix the flours, salt and water together in a bowl. The dough will feel very dry and tight. Once it's come together, tip out onto the bench and kneed for a good 10 minutes. It will feel dry and gritty at the start, but keep working it to develop the gluten and eventually it will become smooth and firm.
3 Roll into a rectangle, wrap in cling-film and chill in the fridge.
4 Place your cold butter between two sheets of greaseproof paper and beat flat.

5 Place the butter on one third of the pastry and fold over, then return to the fridge for two hours.
6 Take the pastry out of the fridge and roll into a rectangle about the length of a sheet of A4 paper but only two thirds of the width.
7 You're now ready to 'turn' or 'book' the pastry. Fold the top third of the pastry into the centre, then fold the bottom third over that. Press together firmly, and stick your finger in it to make a single dent. Put it back in the fridge.
8 Repeat the 'turning' process three times, each time adding a dent so you know where you're up to. Once you've 'turned' it three times, chill over night again.
9 Still with me? You are dedicated!
10 Take out and roll to the required size as fast as you can. Chill again if you've got the space and time. Finally place the pastry on your pie and get it into a screaming hot oven.

Rough puff pastry

So, you've not got time to make classic puff, and even flaky's a bit of a fag. So you're about to get your coat on, go to the shops and buy some puff pastry...

INGREDIENTS
- 220g plain flour
- Pinch of salt
- 75g lard
- 75g butter
- 1 teaspoon of lemon juice

Well, hold on there, and say hello to rough puff. Rough puff is puff pastry that's told the baker to shove it, gone to live with some other woman and smokes and drinks all day. It's the pastry that Slash from Guns'n'Roses would use in the kitchen.

Rough puff still rises, but not as much nor as orderly as classic and flaky. It is, however, a lot easier to make. The difference between it and flaky is that the fat isn't dotted around between the dough layers but is slung in all at once. When finished the dough should have faint streaks of butter visible in it.

METHOD

1 Cut up the fat into small cubes and return to the fridge to firm up again for 15 minutes. Sieve flour and salt together in a bowl and add the fat.

2 Add a few tablespoons of ice-cold water and lemon juice and, using a knife or pair of knives, bring the ingredients together to form a stiff dough.

3 Roll out on a cool floured surface to a rectangle around 25x10cm. Fold the top third down, and the bottom third up on top of that. Make a single mark in the top and pop back in the fridge for ten minutes. Give the dough a quarter-turn, so the edges are facing towards and away from you, roll out again to 25x10cm and fold in the two thirds as before. Make two marks in the dough and pop back in the fridge.

4 Give the dough one last quarter-turn and roll out a final time to 25x10cm. Pop back in the fridge until needed. Then roll into the required shape and use swiftly.

Flaky pastry

Previous page put you off puff, eh? Don't blame you. In that case, sir, can I interest you in flaky pastry? You'll know this from such household favourites as sausage rolls.

INGREDIENTS
- 220g plain flour
- Pinch of salt
- 75g lard
- 75g butter
- 1 teaspoon of lemon juice
- Cold water

Instead of trying to get very fine thin layers of butter between sheets of dough, flaky pastry just requires you to dab blobs of butter or lard between it during each turn. You also mix in a little fat with the dough to begin with.

It doesn't puff up as much as classic puff pastry, and when it does it's in a much more random manner due to the dispersal of the blobs, but it does give you a good result without all the roll, chill, turn ad infinitum of classic puff.

1 Sieve the flour and salt into a bowl and rub in half the lard and half the butter. Add the lemon juice and enough cold water to bring together into a dough – around a few tablespoons should do it. In a separate bowl, mix together the remaining butter and lard.

2 Roll the dough out into a rectangle around 25x10cm.

3 Take a third of the fat mixture and place blobs of it on the top two-thirds of the dough.

4 Fold the un-blobbed bottom third up over the middle, and carefully fold the top half down on to this. Gently squash together and chill for 20 minutes.

5 Roll the dough out again to 25x10cm and repeat the previous stage using another third of the fat. Chill for 20 minutes before doing it again with the final third of the fat mix. Chill again for 20 minutes or more.

6 When needed, roll out to the required size as quickly as you can and use as soon as possible.

Hot-water crust pastry

So far we've covered delicate, tender, melt-in-the-mouth flaky pastries. It's all been 'careful handling' and 'don't overwork the gluten', coupled with more 'chilling' than a Groove Armada gig.

INGREDIENTS

- 225g plain flour
- 225g strong flour
- 150g lard
- 125ml of boiling water
- 1 teaspoon of salt
- 1 teaspoon of sugar

Well all that goes right out the window with the heavy artillery of the pastry world, hot water crust. This hot, fatty bad boy is a strong, firm pastry, able to take a fair bit of stick without blinking; consequently it can hold amounts of filling lesser pastries would go to pieces on. It's best known as the pastry used in the classic pork pie, but traditional raised game pies also make good use of it.

Hot water crust is almost a throwback to the original pastry 'coffins' from the Middle Ages that doubled as a storage container for the filling as well as the receptacle from which to eat it. As its name suggests, it's made from hot water into which you dissolve fat and always lard (though beef dripping works too, I know this because I once picked up the wrong packet in a supermarket), before adding to the flour.

Danger, danger!

Needless to say, like some medieval dungeon keeper you're working with boiling water and scalding hot fat here, so this is probably not a pastry to attempt with the kids charging about the kitchen.

You also need to work quickly with hot water crust. It begins to harden as it cools, so don't hang about. You don't have to keep it in the fridge either, just wrap it in a clean tea towel and keep in a warm place until needed.

1 Sieve the flour into a big glass or ceramic bowl and add the sugar and salt. Have a butter knife standing by.

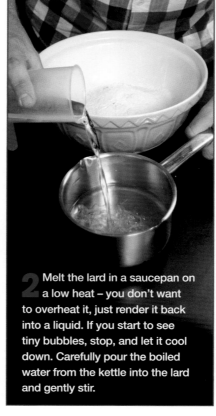

2 Melt the lard in a saucepan on a low heat – you don't want to overheat it, just render it back into a liquid. If you start to see tiny bubbles, stop, and let it cool down. Carefully pour the boiled water from the kettle into the lard and gently stir.

3 Quickly pour this into the bowl containing the flour. Use your knife to mix the dough together, as it'll be way too hot to do it with your hands.

4 When it's cooled to a warm, squidgy texture get your hands in there and begin to work it hard. Don't worry, it can take a bit of a knockabout.

5 Transfer to your bench and kneed for five minutes.

6 Roll out with a rolling pin and remove a quarter for your lid.

7 Gently place the remainder in the pie tin and push to ensure a snug fit.

8 Trim off the excess.

9 Place on your lid and crimp to ensure a good seal.

Suet pudding pastry

You should make a steak and kidney pudding (page 66) once in your life. Pick a cold wintry weekend when you've not much else on, plan ahead, and when you eventually sit down to eat it you'll be richly rewarded.

INGREDIENTS

- 400g self-raising flour
- 200g beef suet
- Pinch of salt
- Around 150ml of water (enough to bring it together as a dough)

A rule of thumb for suet pastry is use around half the weight of suet to flour.

But first you must make the pastry. Though you can bake suet pastry, we mainly steam it in this country to make filled puddings, which can be either savoury or sweet. Once cooked the surface of suet pastry should be crisp, but underneath it should have a light, flaky texture and be almost spongy where some of the juice from the filling has permeated the dough and the suet has rendered out.

WHAT IS SUET?

Suet is the fat found around the internal organs of animals, mainly pork or beef in the UK. The best suet is found round the kidneys. It's a hard, white, crumbly fat with a pleasant flavour and a higher melting point than butter. It comes ready-grated in packets, which makes it much easier to use (must have been a nightmare using it in Victorian times), though some butchers will sell it fresh.

Vegetarian suet is made from palm oil combined with rice flour to resemble real suet. It doesn't have anything near the flavour of real suet though. However, this makes it a better choice for sweet puddings.

If the thought of nursing a steaming pudding for four hours isn't your cup of tea, you can use suet to make dumplings. Just add a little more water to the dough to make it sticky, and roll into small balls about the size of a golf ball (they'll expand a little during cooking). Allow one per person (well, 'allow' seems too strong a word; 'suggest' one per person, but if you can take two dumplings *and* stew, go right ahead).

These can be tucked into a stew for the last half-hour of cooking time, where they'll bob about in the meaty juices getting all nice and soggy underneath while crisping up on top.

1 Sieve the flour and the salt into a bowl.

2 Add the suet and combine thoroughly.

3 Make a well in the centre and add small amounts of water.

4 Slowly bring the dough together with a spoon until you can get your hands in. It's ready when it's not too wet and no flour remains in the bowl. You might need to add a little extra water. Chill for 15 minutes before using.

5 Transfer to your bench and roll out.

6 Cut into a broad circle, ensuring you've a quarter left to form the lid.

7 Position in the pudding basin – ensure no air is trapped.

8 Place your lid on the pudding.

9 Crimp to ensure a good seal. You can then place the plastic lid on ready for steaming.

Cobbler dough mix

Ah the cobbler, the missing link between a loose crumble topping and properly formed pastry. Cobbler dough is actually more like a scone mix, and is made with self-raising flour, often with baking powder added too.

INGREDIENTS
- 225g plain flour
- 4 teaspoons of baking powder
- 100g butter
- Pinch of salt
- 2–4 tablespoons of milk
- Also 60g caster sugar if you're making a sweet cobbler

The finished result is unsurprisingly a scone-like dumpling that's crunchy on the top, yet nice and gooey underneath. A cobbler is one for those with a large appetite. Cobblers allow whatever filling they contain to peak through the gaps in the topping; those little openings are the best place to start with your spoon when it comes to serving.

Cobblers can be savoury as well as sweet, and the dough is able to take on extra flavours within it. So cheese, herbs or spices are a good addition to savoury cobbler batter, while sweet cobblers can take things like dried fruit, chocolate chips or even crystallised ginger.

1 Sieve the flour and salt into a bowl, add the butter cut up into pieces and rub together with your fingers until it resembles golden breadcrumbs. This is the time to add any extra flavours should you want to.

2 Add the milk and gently bring together to make a soft dough.

3 You can either just dollop this on to your filling, or transfer the dough to a work surface and gently roll out to about 2cm thick and cut into round shapes with a pastry cutter or even a glass. These discs can then be placed on the filling.

The art of crimping your edge

FIXING THE LID ON YOUR PIE AND DECORATING IT

Like mortar between two bricks, a wash of beaten egg between the lip and lid of the pie will ensure a good seal. However, a belt and braces approach won't hurt either. Crimping is another way of sealing the pastry lid of the pie to the walls, and you should do that as well as egg wash.

It's vital to get a good seal. If you don't your lid may buckle and distort. Also, you can get what's known in the trade as 'boil out', where the filling forces its way though the seal, and dribbles down the side.

Actually I think a small amount of boil out adds to the character of a pie: as the filling is exposed to direct heat it colours and can give a wonderful *umami* taste. This caused much debate at the annual British Pie Awards (page 180), as technically it's a fault, albeit a tasty one. If too much of the filling boils out, though, it'll burn and turn bitter, as well as make your pie look ugly.

Crimping also allows you to unleash some inner artistic talent, as there are many ways of crimping pies. Pork pies, for example, have a firm, strong crimp, making them almost resemble little crowns.

THE FORK METHOD

Simple and easy. Pressing a fork round the edge of your pie pushes one layer into the other and gives an attractive line around the edge.

PINCH AND PUSH METHOD

With your hand over the top of the pie, pinch the crust together and poke the finger of your other hand into the centre of the pinched pastry.

Letters and adornments

Putting decorative shapes on the lid of your pie isn't just for show, it can help you remember what's in it if you're making it to freeze and eat later. Leaves best signify fruit pies, for instance. Always put on odd numbers of adornments rather than even – for some reason this looks more natural.

Raid the kids' modelling clay set for all sorts of shapes and cutters. You can have great fun with these and make dinosaurs, dolls, spaceships, stars, cars or whatever else they're into at the moment. Obviously, you must always wash such play-tools thoroughly before you use them for pie-making. Buying them new would be even better if you plan to do a lot of pie decorating.

ALPHABET PASTRY CUTTERS

These are great fun and let you write all sorts of words on the top of your pie, from 'I love you' for that special someone to a funny 'Mooooo!' on a beef pie or a rather rude comment for your mates.

WINDOWS AND NEGATIVE SHAPES

You can also cut 'windows' or holes in the lid of your pie. This works really well for things like apple pie, letting you peek in at the filling.

Instead of cutting out your shape from another piece of pastry, cut it out of the lid just before you put it on and then use egg wash to fix the cut-out shape to one side of the hole. Don't make too many or make them too big, however, or you'll compromise the structural integrity of the lid.

Other ingredients you can add to pastry

HERBY PASTRY

Adding dried herbs to your pastry gives an extra flavour hit, but pick something that complements the filling. So think thyme for beef, rosemary for lamb, and tarragon or sage for chicken. Parsley would work in a vegetable pie. And of course there's pepper, which goes with pretty much everything.

POTATO PASTRY

Leftover spuds add an earthy note to pastry. Cold mash is ideal, or the centre of a baked potato. Potatoes with a crust, such as roasties and chips, don't really work. Adding an egg provides further richness and helps bind the potato and flour together.

CHEESE PASTRY

Cheese would be a great addition to a vegetable pie too, but be sure to use a good strong one, so think number four on the cheesy scale. Anything else won't have enough flavour to punch through. Don't add too much, as it may disrupt the fat levels in your pastry.

OTHER TYPES OF PASTRY

There are a few other types of pastry well outside the scope of this book's recipes, but worth mentioning so that you're 'in the know'. Choux (pronounced 'shoe') pastry is found in things like eclairs, profiteroles and other sweet dishes. Of course, chefs wouldn't be chefs if they didn't try to mess with things and do things 'with a twist', so you may occasionally see 'savoury choux' recipes.

Filo pastry is mainly used in Greek, Eastern European and Middle Eastern dishes. This pastry is the thickness of a sheet of paper and often used in layers pasted together with plenty of butter. No one makes this from scratch either, and thankfully there's not a recipe that calls for it in this book.

CHAPTER 3
STOCKS AND SAUCES

So you've decided on which pastry you're using and you've got an idea for the filling; now you just need a sauce. And good sauce starts with good stock. Can you make a cup of tea? Yes? Then you can make stock. It's that easy. It's also dead cheap, uses up leftovers and, most importantly, will make your cooking taste better. Think of making stock as one of those *nice* household tasks; it's certainly more fun than deleting (un)watched programmes from your PVR.

As one of our pie trinity (along with pastry and filling), stock, jus, sauce, gravy or gypper (rhymes with 'zipper') is what keeps our pies moist. All you need for stock is some animal bones, vegetables and water. Sling the lot in the biggest pan you've got and pop on a low heat for three hours. In my freezer I keep a 'bag of bits' which has leek roots and tops, spring onion ends, carrot ends and the ends of onions, as well as celery. This is why I don't have a compost heap – because I put nearly everything into the stockpot. You can put anything you've got on the turn in the fridge in stock, but I wouldn't recommend potato (which will make your stock cloudy) or red onion (which will make it turn a reddish colour).

It's also vitally important that you don't boil stock, as this will cause an emulsion between the fat and the water. Rather just simmer it, let it bubble along. When it's ready, strain it and put it into small containers to cool. Ideally you want lots of containers that hold about 200ml of stock – I've found that a good amount to make pies with. It's worth saving one-pint plastic milk cartons and half-filling these too, as well as any other tubs you come across. Then you can just pop them in the freezer.

Finally a word on roasting bones. Putting bones – whatever the animal – in a screaming hot oven to roast before adding to the stockpot will give you a darker, stronger-flavoured stock. Also, don't add salt to your stocks – rather add it when you use the finished stock in the dishes you want to make.

Chicken stock

HOW TO MAKE CHICKEN STOCK

Throwing away a chicken carcass should be a crime; it also adds insult to (the fatal) injury inflicted on the poor chook you've just scoffed. That bird's bones still have so much flavour to give you, rather than landfill, so make the most of it.

If you've no pressing need for chicken stock in your life right now, pop the carcass in the freezer until you're ready to put it with another one. A two-carcass stock will have much more flavour than a one-bird version. (You might need to break up the birds to fit them in the pot.)

Like beef, roasting the bones will give a darker colour and more robust flavour. If you're after something more delicate, use as is.

You can add more chicken reinforcements to your carcass – chicken wings are dead cheap, and their high gelatine content makes for a great sticky, flavoursome stock.

INGREDIENTS

- 1 or 2 chicken carcasses
- 6 chicken wings (optional)
- 2 carrots roughly chopped
- 1 stick of celery
- 6 whole peppercorns
- 2 bay leaves
- 2 large onions quartered
- Small bunch of parsley stalks
- 2 litres of water

METHOD

1 Place ingredients in a large saucepan and add two litres of cold water.
2 Place on a low heat and allow to simmer for three hours.
3 Strain and portion into containers.

CHICKEN STOCK ANOTHER WAY

Once the stars aligned and fate delivered to me three *poulet de Bresse* chicken carcasses. These are some of the most pampered chickens in the world, living long, happy lives in France before they arrive on our tables; they're the Rolls-Royce of chickens. Consequently this bounty required special treatment, so I did an overnight stock. This is exactly the same as above, but you place the pan in a low oven around 90°C to reduce overnight.

REMOUILLAGE

After you've strained your stock and the bones and veg have given their best, you can still use them to produce a second-rate stock. The French call this a *remouillage*. It won't be as strong or flavoursome as the first stock, but it does have uses.

DOUBLE STOCK

You can turn the chicken-ness up to 11 with this technique. Instead of adding two litres of water to your carcasses, you add two litres of a previously made chicken stock. Cook it exactly the same way as above, strain and enjoy. This is where the *remouillage* outlined above comes in handy.

ADDITIONS

Of course, the above recipe is just for a basic stock. You can always tweak flavours depending on your intended final use. So try adding herbs like tarragon, sage leaves and rosemary. If you're using your stock in a spicier context, then chuck in a sliced fresh chilli and maybe a thumb of fresh ginger. You could also replace the parsley with coriander. Finally, any dregs of white wine you've got left over can also be added.

OTHER BIRDS

Pheasant, duck and turkey can all be made into stock. You might have trouble finding a pan big enough to take a turkey carcass whole, so either break it up or just use half, freezing the other half for later.

Beef stock

HOW TO MAKE BEEF STOCK

It's always worth buying beef on the bone if you can as it provides not only flavour and structure during the initial cooking but also makes amazing stock.

Your butcher may even give you some bones for free. It helps if you buy something else too; don't just walk in and demand bones.

For beef stock I like to add a single petal from a star anise. Trust me, this'll give an extra perfumed note to the stock but won't overpower it.

If you want a really dark stock, or the bones are fresh, you might want to roast them first. Put the oven on full whack, and pop them in for 15 minutes.

INGREDIENTS

- Beef bones – whatever you can get your hands on, the more the merrier; any beef trimmings, and if you really want to any beef bits left on your dining plates
- 2 large carrots
- 2 sticks of celery
- 1 large onion
- Parsley including stalks (optional)
- 6 peppercorns
- 1 'petal' from a star anise
- 2 bay leaves
- 3 litres of water

Cooking time: four hours minimum, longer if you've got time. It's even better if done overnight.

METHOD

1 Place all the ingredients in a large pan and pour in a kettle of freshly boiled water. Top up with cold water if needed. Put on a low heat on the back burner and leave it, lid off, for four to five hours.
2 The oven method: put your stock in the oven on a low heat (say 60°C) overnight. Your kitchen will smell amazing the next morning.
3 Once all the ingredients in the stock are looking like they've given all they have to give, strain and leave to cool before decanting into containers.

OTHER MEATS

The recipe above applies just as much for other meats like pork, lamb and veal. Lamb stock will make any lamb dish like shepherd's pie (page 116) taste much better. Pork stock, meanwhile, is great in a pork pie (page 73), and if you really get into stocks (warning: it can become addictive) then make a rabbit version for rabbit pie (page 100).

Fish stock

HOW TO MAKE FISH STOCK

Stocks made with meat get better the longer you reduce them. With fish, the opposite is true. Cook a fish stock for too long and you'll end up with glue.

You can make fish stock from fish bones, but unless you've got access to a good fishmonger the opportunity to get hold of enough bones is limited. Far better is to use bits of fresh fish that nobody wants, things like heads. Salmon and cod heads can be picked up cheaply, even in some supermarkets, but it's far better to seek out a decent fishmonger. Indeed, if you buy some actual fish from them they'll probably throw in the heads for free. Your other option is to buy whole fish and have the fishmonger take it to bits for you, and keep the carcass for stock.

White fish and salmon (despite it being classed as an oily fish) are the best for making stock. I wouldn't recommend the more oily fish, like mackerel. Shellfish can be added to a 'fish' stock too – shells of prawns, crabs, scallops and mussels are all fair game, though they'll give a slightly different flavour.

INGREDIENTS

- 1 or 2 cod or salmon heads
- Any other assorted fishy bits (prawns, shellfish etc)
- 1 leek
- 1 onion (studded with one clove)
- 1 glass of white wine
- 1 handful of parsley

METHOD

1 Place ingredients snugly in a pan and top up with cold water.
2 Bring up to rapid simmer for no longer than 30 minutes.
3 Strain and cool quickly.

Unlike chicken and beef stocks, in which your aim is to reduce and concentrate the essence and flavour of the meat, a fish stock should be clear, light and have a delicate nautical air. If your stock is thick, cloudy and has a strong fishy smell you've overdone it.

OTHER ADDITIONS

A shot of Pernod adds a floral aniseed note to a fish stock, or you could add half a bulb of fennel. A tablespoon of double cream or crème fraîche takes things from being a stock to being a sauce, and from here you can go anywhere, adding fresh dill if your pie features salmon, or perhaps some finely chopped chives.

Vegetable stock

HOW TO MAKE VEGETABLE STOCK

Vegetable stock is the cheapest of all stocks to make, as it uses ingredients you can probably pick up for pence or that are on the turn in your fridge. The key is to use a good range and quantity of vegetables; like a party with too few guests, a single carrot, onion and leek just won't be able to give off enough flavour to make a stock worthwhile, so put in a good amount. Again, everything's fair game for inclusion except red onion and potatoes. The former will turn your stock red (though sometimes this is desirable), the latter will make it cloudy and mealy.

INGREDIENTS

- 3 onions
- 3 carrots
- 2 leeks
- 2 celery sticks
- 1 courgette
- 2 tomatoes
- 1 fennel bulb
- 1 pepper
- 1 bunch of parsley
- 1 bay leaf
- 1 teaspoon of peppercorns

Button mushrooms, chilli, lemongrass, pepper offcuts and indeed anything else you can get your hands on can all be added to vegetable stock to take it in a different direction depending on your final usage. Mushrooms add an earthy *umami* note while spices take things out to Asia. Too much broccoli, cabbage and other brassicas can overpower your stock, so balance them carefully. This is a great time to delve into your 'bits bag' in the freezer and see if there's any other bits kicking about that you could use.

TIPS FOR PREPARATION

Chopping the vegetables into large chunks rather than chucking them in whole increases the surface area and lets more flavour out. Don't chop too fine, however, as it'll turn to mush. Another tip is to lightly roast or sauté the vegetables, which will give you a deeper, caramelised flavour.

Don't underestimate vegetable stock – a good one can outflank a poorly made meat version with ease. I've seen commercial kitchens where nearly every scrap of vegetable offcut goes into a boiler the size of a bathtub with a tap at the bottom, and is simmered for days. What comes out is a cheap-as-chips flavourful stock that works with just about anything.

METHOD

1 Place all the ingredients in a large pan and cover with cold water. Bring up to a slow boil then turn down and simmer for 1 to 2 hours, skimming any scum that rises to the surface.
2 Strain out the spent vegetables and use.
3 You can reduce further by returning the liquid to the pan and simmering for another hour.

Jelly stock

Jelly stocks are used primarily in pork pies to fill the gap between pastry and the chopped meat filling which contracts on cooking. They also form an airtight barrier to protect the meat and keep it moist.

For proper pork pies you need a pork-based stock, and in my book this has to include pigs' trotters. They add both flavour and the required wobble once cooled, and they contain loads of gelatine. However, other animal extremities contain gelatine too, such as cow's feet and chicken wings, and any stock made with these will also set to a wobble.

But let's concern ourselves with the pork version. Here's what you need:

A cheat's jelly stock

If you're in a real rush, or you can't get your hands on some decent pigs' trotters, you can add 4–6 pre-soaked and squeezed sheets of leaf gelatine to any hot stock and stir until it's dissolved. I say you *can* do this, but that doesn't mean you should, as it won't have the genuine sticky pork flavour of jelly stock made from scratch.

INGREDIENTS

- 1–2 pigs' trotters (you'll have to go to a butcher for these as, along with pigs' heads they're never seen in supermarkets as they might remind shoppers that they're, you know, eating an actual animal)
- Assorted pork bones (these can be from the shoulder, hock, leg, anything you can beg, steal or borrow from your butcher)
- 2 onions
- 2 carrots
- Teaspoon of peppercorns
- A few sprigs of parsley
- A few sprigs of thyme
- 1 bay leaf

METHOD

1 Place all the ingredients in your largest saucepan and cover with cold water. Bring slowly to the boil then turn down to a gentle simmer for 3 hours. Do not use a lid.
2 After 3 hours, when everything should be falling to bits, strain through a colander into a large bowl to remove the bigger bits, then through a fine sieve back into the saucepan to get out any smaller bits.
3 Keep warm until needed or chill, freeze and then reheat.

Sauces and roux

INGREDIENTS

- 50g butter
- 45g flour
- 300ml milk

ROUX THE DAY

If you learn to make one proper sauce in your life, learn to make a roux (pronounced 'roo'). From this you can make béchamel, one of the great French chef Escoffier's five mother sauces, from which many more daughter sauces can be made. History fans may like to know that it's named after the Marquis de Béchamel, financier of Louis XIV.

The beauty of this sauce is that you can adjust pretty much everything about it: pull back on the flour and it's a pouring sauce; add a bit more, and you've got a thicker sauce for things like chicken and mushroom pie (page 92), as well as fish pie (page 104).

'Equal quantities of fat and flour mixed over a low heat' is how you make a roux. However, I tend to favour slightly more fat than flour, with butter as the traditional fat used. You can also gild the lily by first simmering an onion studded with a few cloves in the milk beforehand, to impart more flavour.

METHOD

1 Gently melt the butter in a saucepan until liquid.

2 Add the flour (sieving it in with a small sieve will help it stop clumping together, I find), which will foam up.

3 Stir the mixture vigorously with a wooden spoon. It will clump together, but keep stirring – you want to cook the flour in the butter.

4 When it's settled down a bit and returned to a more liquid state, add cold milk a bit at a time. It will immediately turn solid again – just keep gently stirring. As the sauce becomes liquid you may want to switch to using a whisk. You now have a béchamel sauce.

5 After a few minutes taste the sauce. If it tastes of flour, add more milk and keep cooking.

6 When you're satisfied you can either add more flavourings or keep until needed. Just cover the saucepan with cling film to stop a skin forming on your béchamel.

USES FOR ROUX SAUCES

A roux is a blank canvas that can take further flavours. Adding milk gives us a béchamel sauce. We can then add additional flavours:

Cheese

Adding cheese to a béchamel makes your classic cheese sauce; a good handful should do it. It's best to use a strong cheese so that the flavour comes through. Also bear in mind that the cheese will thicken the sauce as it melts, so you may want to start off with a thinner roux. Cheddar, parmesan and even Stilton are good, or a nutty Continental cheese.

Herbs

Parsley sauce is a traditional English sauce served with gammon and white fish. You can infuse the milk with mace and parsley stalks prior to adding to the sauce. It's lovely poured over a bit of mash.

Mushrooms

Finely diced and fried mushrooms can be added to béchamel to create mushroom sauce. Try to use wild or porcini ones – button mushrooms have very little flavour that'll just get lost in the sauce.

Mustard

A blob of mustard gives béchamel extra oomph, while freshly grated horseradish takes it to level 11.

A BROWN ROUX

Sometimes you may see a recipe that calls for something called a brown roux. This just means you cook the butter and flour mix for longer until it starts to go a light nutty brown colour.

OTHER LIQUIDS INSTEAD OF MILK

You can also add meat, fish or vegetable stock instead of milk, which will give a browner, more flavourful sauce – it'll be a little runnier, mind. White wine can also be added alongside milk to make a white wine sauce. Cider or beer can be added to a brown roux to make a nice sauce for pork too. A splash of Pernod will add an aniseed flavour for a fish sauce. I'd avoid other spirits, though.

TOMATO SAUCE

Another sauce you should have in your repertoire is a simple tomato sauce. This is a doddle to make, consisting of a chopped onion sweated with garlic in a pan, to which you add a tin of plum tomatoes and a pinch of dried herbs. Let the whole lot cook down gently before leaving to cool. You can keep it in the fridge for a few days, or freeze into batches.

It can be used on pizza, in meatball pie (page 83), as a pasta sauce, or diluted with hot water to form an instant soup.

CHAPTER 4

MEAT PIES

Right, this is what it's all about, gents. Enough with the pep and prep talk; are your hands cool, your mind focused and your kitchen cleaned and ready? Good. Then let's get some cooking on the go. And what better place to start, than with meat pies. If you only learn to make one pie from this book, make it a good meaty one, perhaps the steak and ale, or oxtail and beef cheek. Think about it – that rich gravy, those tender chunks of beef, that golden pastry. *That's* what we're aiming for.

Many of the following pie recipes use either stewing or braising steak, offal and offcuts, mince, or leftovers from larger roasted joints. None of these are particularly expensive, but it's worth spending a bit extra getting good quality meat for your pies; it'll have more flavour and a better texture. Look for beef that's dryer, and has a deep, rich, almost purple colour rather than a bright red wet one. Remember, age equals flavour.

Making pies from leftover roasted joints was how things were done in the old days. It's always worth buying a bigger joint, with one eye on tomorrow. Lamb, pork and beef joint leftovers can all be made into pies. Just allow to cool and chop or flake into bite-size pieces.

Tips for handling meat

Which is the dirtiest thing in your house? The loo, right? Wrong. It's more than likely your kitchen sink. According to the NHS, studies show that the kitchen contains the most germs in the home. Indeed, one study found that the kitchen sink contains 100,000 times more germs than the bathroom, with E. coli, campylobacter and salmonella being the main dangers.

Therefore the first rule of cooking, gentlemen, is wash your hands: before, during and after your stint at the stove. You know this I'm sure, but it's amazing how, in the heat of battle, this simple action gets forgotten (the second rule of cooking, by the way, is to ensure the cook has a drink; at least, it is in our house). If you've ever had food poisoning, it's not nice.

WASHING

Raw meat is fine to handle, but you just need to be aware of what it's touched, be that pans, chopping boards, tongs or knives. Professional kitchens have different coloured chopping boards for different ingredients to help minimise cross-contamination (red for raw meat, blue for fish, yellow for cooked meat, brown for vegetables, green for fruits and salad, and white for pastry and dairy). While six different chopping boards might be a bit much for the average domestic kitchen, you can at least take a leaf out of this book and have one board for raw food and one for cooked. I'd recommend having a bigger board for raw meat work – taking apart a chicken takes up more room than dicing a carrot or chopping an onion.

Clean chopping boards regularly with anti-bacterial spray. Plastic ones can go in the dishwasher; wooden ones need a good scrub with a scourer. If your boards are getting a bit damaged, take a knife and scrape across it or, better still, take it out to the shed and get some sandpaper on it. Butchers regularly do this, which results in the curvy blocks you used to see in their shops. You want to remove any cuts, grooves, nooks and crannies where bacteria can hide and breed.

HANDS

Remember to clean your tap handles regularly too. There's no point turning on a tap with raw meaty hands, washing then clean, then turning off the tap with your clean hands. You may just transfer any bacteria from the tap handle back to your hands.

I try to be meticulous about hygiene. So if I've used a small knife to cut open a packet of meat, that knife will be washed before it's used for anything that isn't raw meat work.

PERFECT PREP

The way I like to work is to do all the raw meat work in one go if possible, then clean down before attempting anything else. It's especially important to keep raw meat away from any ingredients that won't be cooked, like bread, salad and fruit, so don't break down that chicken next to the fruit bowl.

SPONGES

Kitchen sponges and cloths can harbour all sorts of things, so change these regularly, every week at least. If one is particularly dirty but still fairly new you can put it through the dishwasher.

TONGS

Tongs are great for moving raw meat around, but once it's in place and cooking wash them or use another pair for cooked food.

Buy a meat thermometer

Once the preserve of caterers, commercial kitchens and chefs, digital meat thermometers cost less than a fiver nowadays. With one of these you can see if the internal temperature of your meat is over the recommended 75°C (for 30 seconds minimum). This is enough to kill any harmful bacteria and parasites.

Handling raw meat

Keep raw meat sealed in either a container or a bag and at the bottom of the fridge where it can't drip on anything else. (This goes back to a time when many fridges had bars for shelves; most these days are glass. The rule still applies, though, as the bottom of the fridge is the coldest, which will inhibit bacteria.) You should always let your meat come up to room temperature before cooking it. Going from a cold fridge to a hot oven won't cook it all the way through.

FREEZING AND DEFROSTING MEAT

Bulk buying a bargain and storing in the freezer is a good thing. However, you should always defrost meat in the fridge. Also make sure it's on a plate or in a bowl. Defrosted meat will look more 'bloody' because of the addition of melted water. Liquid has an amazing way of getting out of any packet, and it's disheartening to say the least to open your fridge and see a pool of blood dripping on to the salad tray beneath.

Also, if you're going to freeze mince you might want to take it out of the packet and remove the nappy of tissue paper that's there to soak up any excess blood. I've found this difficult to remove from defrosted mince; it ends up sticking to it, and tears as you try to pull it off.

CHICKEN

Do *not* wash your chicken (or any other meat, for that matter) under the kitchen tap – all you succeed in doing is splashing raw chicken juice over your sink and worktop. This practice was once recommended when poultry was slaughtered in back yards, and might still have mud, pooh and other things on it, but meat you buy today has already been washed and cleaned.

PORK

Once food safety advice was to cook pork until it resembled shoe leather. This, we were told, was the only way to kill the larvae of roundworm, which can cause trichinosis (basically a very bad tum). Then someone had the bright idea of actually cleaning up pork production as well as treating the animals to eradicate roundworm. Consequently in 2011 the USDA lowered the recommended internal cooking temperature of cooked pork by 15°F. Chefs in the US and here in the UK rejoiced that pork could be served 'pink'. However, the UK Food Standards Agency still recommend cooking pork thoroughly until any juices run clear.

BEEF

Just because it's the only meat we eat raw (in steak tartare) doesn't mean hygiene rules don't apply. Always wash your hands after handling beef. Having said that, beef does have a lovely texture, and running your fingers over it, checking the firmness and prodding the fat helps you understand that this was once a muscle of a cow.

LAMB

Same rules apply as other meats: wash hands and equipment after handling.

HANDLING COOKED MEAT

Cooked meat is much easier to handle, but should be kept in the fridge on a separate shelf from raw meat. If you can, keep your cooked meat in a container or wrapped in a bag, as a dry, cold fridge can dry out cooked meat.

How to mince properly

Minced meat is used in a great many of the pies in this book, from a fluffy potato-topped shepherd's pie to the solid classic that's a Melton Mowbray pork variety, so it's worth getting mince right.

COOKING MINCE

Most beef mince you see in the supermarkets these days contains loads of fat and water. When you tip it in the pan, this liquid comes out and your mince effectively boils rather than browns, which leaves it grey and chewy.

So first off, look for good quality lean mince with a low fat percentage (many packets now state this). Another tip is to always use coarse ground mince: this will have more structure and less surface area, which will help reduce fat rendering. I also think it has a better texture in the mouth.

Don't add loads of oil or other fat either, just a few drops to stop the meat sticking initially. It'll soon render out its own fat. Ensure your pan is big enough, and fry the mince in batches on a very high heat.

MINCE AND GRIND

If you're really serious about meat and mincing, then consider investing in a domestic meat grinder. You've three options here: hand-powered, a kitchen mixer attachment, or a bespoke machine. Hand-powered ones range from £20–£40 and clamp to your work surface. They're OK for mincing up small amounts in batches, but be prepared to put in some elbow grease. If you own a Kenwood or KitchenAid mixer you can buy an attachment that clamps on the front and uses the power of the motor to grind the meat. Finally, for the man who has everything, there's a standalone electric meat grinder. Lakeland do one for about £100. With this you can mince meat not only for pies, but for burgers too. There's even an attachment and kit that lets you make your own sausages. The joy of this is that you know exactly what's gone into them, and can tweak the flavours at will. Put one on your Christmas wish list.

Flouring meat, marinating meat

FLOURING YOUR MEAT

Many recipes call for meat to be dusted in flour before searing in a pan. There are a few schools of thought as to why you should do this. Some say it helps thicken the sauce later on, and that it forms a crust that protects the meat and helps with the caramelisation. You can add additional flavourings to the flour beyond salt and pepper, perhaps a teaspoon of dried mustard or dried herbs and spices.

Of course, there are others who think you shouldn't flour meat at all, and should just rely on the natural sugars to form a crust.

Personally I think that flouring meat helps remove some of the moisture that you find in much meat today.

If you're going to flour your meat here's how to do it properly:

- Place a small amount of flour on a plate and season well.
- Add any extra flavourings you might want depending on your recipe.
- Always add the meat in small batches, perhaps 8 to 10 pieces max.
- Coat them in flour then dust off any excess using a sieve.
- Transfer to the hot waiting pan immediately to brown.

If you leave the flour on for too long it'll start to go claggy and pasty as it draws moisture from the meat, then when the meat hits the fat the flour will form clumps of batter, which you don't want. Your floured meat shouldn't look like Turkish Delight, but should just have a light dusting.

MARINATING MEAT

Marinating adds extra flavour and can also tenderise the meat. There are three main ways of marinating: dry rub, wet marinade, and what I call 'gloopy marinade'. As you'd expect, dry rub calls for dried herbs, seeds and spices to be rubbed on to the meat, and common ingredients are paprika, salt, pepper, sugar, chilli powder, onion powder, coriander seeds, cumin and mustard. These are used mainly in US-style BBQ cooking; the rub stays on the meat when it's grilled over coals, and the fat cooks the rub, imparting flavour.

Wet marinades see meat submerged in liquids for long periods of time. So beef can be bathed in beer, pork in cider, and chicken in wine, such as the classic *coq au vin*. In most cases the marinade goes on to become part of the sauce for the dish, so don't throw it away (it goes without saying that you shouldn't drink it either!).

'Gloopy marinades', as I call them, see the meat coated in thicker sauces, often yoghurt-based. Many Asian recipes call for this treatment. You're looking for something with a decent acidic content to help tenderise the meat.

If you've marinated your meat you don't need to flour it, but I'd recommend removing it from the marinade and letting it dry out a bit before browning.

Browning meat, deglazing the pan

As I intimated in the introduction, to make a good pie filling you sometimes have to make a stew first. Browning the meat is crucial to that; it provides flavour, and I think it helps the meat keep its structure. Again, much like flouring your meat, you want to brown it in small batches. Chucking a whole load of floured meat in the pan will cool it right down, there won't be enough room, and it'll result in grey-looking meat.

Get your pan hot, but not full whack. I tend to favour a plain oil like sunflower or vegetable. Don't use olive oil, it's a waste. You can also add a knob of butter, which will help give colour more quickly, but be careful you don't have the heat too high.

Place the meat in gently, making sure it's in contact with some oil, and don't push and pull it about – leave it completely still.

You can tell when it's ready, as it'll come away from the pan; if it's still sticking, it's not ready. You want it to have a charred, caramelised surface – technically known as the Maillard reaction, science fans. (Contrary to what you might have read elsewhere, this doesn't 'seal in the flavour'.) Then remove with a slotted spoon to a clean plate and do the next batch.

After a few batches, you may need to wipe out the pan with a piece of kitchen roll to get rid of any excess fat and add more oil. Whatever you do you should leave any sticky bits on the bottom of the pan. These will provide flavour.

DEGLAZING THE PAN

Another key stage in filling-making is deglazing the pan. This means adding a liquid to your pan to lift off all those lovely bits that are stuck to it. If you've marinated your meat in wine or beer you can add this now. It'll sizzle, but that's OK. Rub around the pan with a spatula to make sure you've got all the bits up. You then add back in all your other bits – meat, vegetables, onions and such. Bring it up to a boil then slam in the oven and forget about it for a few hours.

Beef and ale pie

This is it, the big one. This recipe, more a technique really, was given to me by Chris, my local butcher. It's a long process, that's for sure – we're not in the world of the quick midweek supper here. It's a two-stage, two-day process, but believe me it's well worth it. Also, you don't have to tend it, just give it a nudge now and again on the hour to see how it's doing.

INGREDIENTS

- 500g skirt steak
- 1kg braising steak
- Beef shin bone (or any other bone)
- 2 large onions (or 4 medium ones)
- 3 large carrots
- 1 bottle of porter, stout or dark ale (around 300ml)
- 200ml of water
- 3 tablespoons of seasoned flour
- 2 teaspoons of cornflour
- 1 petal from a 'flower' of star anise
- Salt and pepper

The method involves two types of beef: skirt steak and chuck or braising steak. Skirt is the traditional meat used in Cornish pasties (see page 136) and has a feathered texture. In this recipe it breaks down into tiny individual strands to give a thick, meaty gravy.

Braising steak is added later – this will remain whole in the pie, so you want mouth-sized pieces. The last ingredient is bones. Ask your butcher for any beef bones he might have. If he's a good butcher he should have some. You may have to give him a bit of notice, mind. It's the marrow in the bones that you're after.

The choice of ale is important too. You need something dark with depth and flavour. I'm currently a fan of Meantime Brewery's Chocolate Porter, but a stout would work just as well. This recipe makes a lot of filling (that's the idea), and you might not need it all for your pie today. Use what you need and freeze the rest, where it'll quietly wait ready for that midweek supper.

METHOD
Stage one

1 Chop half of your onions, add to the largest pan you have along with the bones and the skirt steak.

2 Pour the bottle of beer over it. Top up with water if you think it needs it. Put on the hob on the lowest heat imaginable and leave for 4–5 hours. Check on the hour to see it's all right.

3 After five hours, remove the bones and any gristle that may have come off them. They should be clean. Turn up the heat a bit to reduce.

Stage two

4 Preheat the oven to 120°C. Peel the carrots, chop into large chunks and chop the remaining onion(s) into a dice.

5 In a separate casserole pan, sweat onions and carrots gently until tender. (If you've only got one pan and you used it for stage one, tip that out into a mixing bowl, dry with kitchen roll, and brown the braising steak in that.)

6 Remove into a bowl and then flour the braising steak. You don't need to brown it for this recipe, just chuck it in.

7 Add the meat, the vegetables, star anise and enough of the meaty gravy from stage one to the pan to just cover the ingredients. Season well with pepper (we'll add the salt towards the end) and place in the oven at 120°C for another three hours.

By now your kitchen, indeed your whole house, should smell amazing. The dog will be going bananas. You'll no doubt be sick of the sight of this stew. That's fine, because you don't need it now, it's for tomorrow. When the beef is falling apart and the sauce thick, it's done. Add the salt. Leave to cool down and store in the fridge.

MAKING THE PIE

Pastry time! For me, this pie needs light, crumbly shortcrust (see page 32), but you could use rough puff or flaky if you prefer. You've some options here on construction too; either make lots of individual pies, or one big one for the table. You *can* make a single crust large one, but I think a filling of this calibre deserves a double crust.

I've even seen some individual pies with a shortcrust bottom and a puff pastry top. If you do make single ones, you'll need to adjust the cooking times. What follows is for a double crust large pie. See page 19 for pastry amounts for specific tin sizes.

1 Make enough pastry to double-line your tin. You want the bottom piece to be a little thicker than the lid.
2 Roll out the lid. Brush the lip of the pie with egg wash and lay the lid on top. Seal the edges with a crimp of your choice and brush with more egg wash.
3 It'll keep like this in the fridge for another hour or so. Don't leave it too long, mind. When needed, place in a preheated oven at 190°C for 20 to 25 minutes before turning down to 150°C for a final 10 minutes. Leave to stand for 10 minutes after cooking. Serve with mashed potatoes and red cabbage.

Steak and kidney pudding

This, gents, is one of England's greatest dishes, yet it's actually not that old. Mrs Beeton gives us the first written recipe, which she says came to her from a lady in Sussex, a county that was once famous for its puddings (Sussex pond pudding being the other well-known example).

INGREDIENTS

- 800g braising steak
- 400g trimmed and prepared kidney
- 1 large onion
- A few slugs of Worcestershire sauce
- 400ml of beef stock
- The leaves off two sprigs of thyme
- 400ml of flavourful beer
- Small handful of dried mushrooms soaked in warm water (optional)
- Four tablespoons of flour for dusting the meat
- A few sprigs of thyme
- A few big grinds of pepper
- A pinch of salt
- Tablespoon of vegetable oil

Essentially it's like every other pie, in that you make a stew filling first and then, once cooled, encase it in a pastry crust. However, the crust is made with suet (see page 40), and because the pudding is steamed rather than cooked in an oven the result is a softer, sponge-like crust.

The choice of kidney is important too. A bad kidney will taste of pee – I'm not really selling this to you, am I? So try and get really fresh kidneys, as, like all offal, they deteriorate rapidly. While cows' kidneys might seem the first choice, they can have a very strong taste. Veal kidneys will be less harsh, and lamb's more delicate still. Some tinned steak and kidney pies (you know to what product I'm referring) use pork kidneys, which are the cheapest.

My advice is start with lamb and work your way up to ox. Please don't leave out the kidneys, though – you need that slightly earthy, offal tang that they give (interestingly Mrs Beeton actually recommends adding oysters, as they were cheaper than meat in those days, though that would make the filling taste totally different).

Whichever kidney you use, you'll need to remove the hard, white, central core of each one, as well as any membrane. Cut the kidney in half and remove the core with a sharp knife. It's the core that, if left in, can contribute the – ahem – pee-like taste (wait, come back!).

There's two ways to make a 'Kate and Sidney' pudding. One sees the raw filling added to the bowl and the other way calls for the filling to be made first, then left to cool before being added. Personally I favour the latter. It means a two-stage process, but will give you a much more consistent result. You can also cook more filling than you need and freeze it.

This recipe is enough for a 1.5-litre pudding bowl. You want to make the filling the day before if possible.

TO MAKE THE FILLING

1. Add the oil to a casserole pan and put on a high heat.
2. Flour the meat in small batches and brown in the pan (see page 61), then set aside.
3. Add the onion and herbs to the pan and soften.
4. Return the meat to the pan and add the stock and the beer. Add the mushrooms if using at this stage.
5. Place in a low oven (120°C) and cook for 3 hours.

TO MAKE THE PASTRY

Puddings use suet pastry (see page 40). The main difference from, say, shortcrust is that it uses self-raising flour rather than plain. You can use plain if you add baking powder to it – follow the instruction on page 28. You'll need about 600g of suet pastry.

6. Once you've made it, chill it for at least 30 minutes.
7. Butter your pudding dish.
8. Cut off about a quarter of it and set to one side (for the lid).
9. Roll the remaining pastry out on a floured surface into a circular shape about 20cm wide and 1cm thick.
10. Carefully line your dish with the disc of pastry, making sure it's flush with the dish. You want it to come about 1cm over the lip. Roll out the remaining quarter to form your lid.
11. Add your cooled filling mix, then trim off the 1cm lip, brush with water, and pop the lid on. You can then trim the excess off and press gently down to get a good seal.

PAPER, FOIL AND STRING

Traditionally a pleated piece of foil and greaseproof paper would be tied on to the top of the pudding bowl, but if you buy plastic pudding basins (and you should) they now come with a plastic lid, which is *much* easier and involves far less faffing about.

COOKING

12 Put the pudding in a large pan with a lid big enough to hold it, and fill with water until it comes halfway up the side of the basin. Put the lid on the pan and simmer for about 3 hours. You might need to top up the water midway through.

13 After 3 hours remove (careful, it'll be hot) and leave to stand for 5 minutes before taking off the pudding basin lid.

14 Turn out on to a warm plate and take to the table with a loud 'Ta-dah!' Break it gently with a spoon and portion out one of the best dishes you can ever make.

Classic minced beef pies

I can't think of a cheaper beef pie than this. It also happens to be dead easy to make. The filling is similar to that used in a cottage pie. My advice is to bulk-buy some good quality mince, make a huge vat of this, and freeze it into portions. You can then whip it out and encase it in pastry or top with potato (page 115). If you're really dedicated you could make your own mince (see page 59). This recipe is for a large 9in/22cm double crust pie. The filling would make 3/4 individual pies. For a single crust pie you won't need as much pastry (freeze the leftovers), but you may need a pie bird.

INGREDIENTS

For the filling
- 500g mince
- 200ml beef stock
- 2 onions
- Tablespoon of vegetable oil
- 1 stick of celery
- 1 carrot
- Large handful of frozen peas (optional)
- Salt and pepper
- 1 teaspoon of tomato purée

For the pastry
- 400g plain flour
- 100g butter
- 100g lard
- Pinch of salt
- A few tablespoons of cold water
- 1 beaten egg or milk to seal the edge and glaze

TO MAKE THE FILLING

1 Bring your meat out of the fridge and remove from the packet – pat dry with kitchen roll if needed. Chop your onions, carrots and celery into a dice (you can use other diced vegetables such as swede, parsnip or potato to bulk out your pie).

2 On a high-ish heat, add the oil to the pan and begin browning the mince in small batches. Only move it when it starts to brown and comes away easily. When browned nearly all over, remove to a side plate.

3 When all the mince is done, add the vegetables and cook in any remaining fat or oil until the onion is translucent (about 8–10 minutes).

4 Add the tomato purée, the stock and the meat and any juices back to the pan and combine.

5 Add the seasoning and simmer, lid off, for 30 minutes, stirring occasionally.

6 When the filling is thickened and reduced you can remove from the heat. If your filling looks a little runny, blend a teaspoon of cornflour in cold water and add to thicken it.

7 Add the peas if you want to. These will cook in the residual heat as well as when baked in the pie.

8 Let the filling cool right down before you try to fill a pie case with it.

TO MAKE THE PASTRY

While your filling is cooling down make the pastry.

9 Make the shortcrust in the method described on page 32. Chill, then roll out to fit your tin. Combine the leftovers if you need to and re-roll out to cut your pie lids.

10 Add the filling to the lined pastry case to just over three-quarters full – you don't want to overfill it.

11 Brush the lip with beaten egg and pop the lid on. Crimp with your fingers or a fork to get a good seal.

12 Brush with the beaten egg and put in a preheated oven at 180°C for 25/30 minutes until the crust looks golden brown.

13 Take out and allow to cool a little before serving.

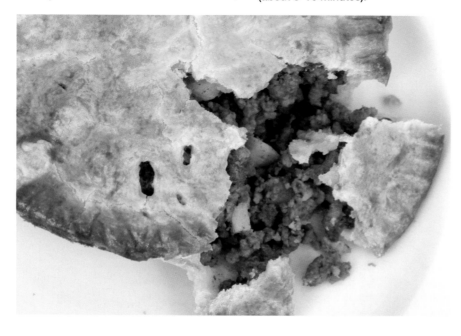

Norfolk plough pudding

In medieval times the blessing of the plough on the first Monday after Twelfth Night (early January) marked the end of Christmas festivities and the start of that year's farming. Naturally, food and lots of drink were part of the original celebrations, so as well as ale there was often a huge pudding made. The practice had fallen out of favour by the Elizabethan age, but saw something of a revival in the Folk movement of the 1970s, particularly in places like Sussex, Worcestershire and Norfolk. So why not join in this fine tradition by making a pudding and blessing your lawnmower?

In times past I'm sure the plough pudding was filled with whatever folks could get, but these days all recipes call for pork sausage meat. It's essentially a cross between a sausage roll and a steamed pudding. This recipe is enough for a two-pint basin.

INGREDIENTS

For the filling

- 750g sausage meat or minced pork belly
- A few finely chopped sage leaves
- Lots of ground black pepper
- 50g smoked bacon lardons (or 6 thick streaky bacon rashers finely diced if you can't get lardons)
- 1 medium onion finely diced
- A few tablespoons of water to bind
- Around 50ml of water or stock

For the pastry

A plough pudding is made with suet pastry, just like a steak and kidney. Follow the instructions on page 40. You'll need about 600g. Once made chill for 30 minutes.

- 240g self-raising flour
- A small pinch of sea salt
- ½ teaspoon of freshly ground black pepper
- 70g of suet, shredded (try and use beef suet)
- Enough water to combine into a dough (around 150ml)

METHOD

1 Finely chop the onion and combine with the sausage meat, chopped bacon and sage. Season well and add a little water to bind together.
2 Butter your pudding bowl.
3 Cut off a third of your pastry and reserve it for the lid of the pudding.
4 Roll the remaining pastry out on a floured surface into a circular shape about 20cm wide and 1cm thick.
5 Carefully line your dish with the disc of pastry, making sure it's flush with the dish. You want it to come about 1cm over the lip.
6 Add the filling mix, making sure there are no gaps. Pour a small amount of the stock over. This is just to keep it moist and stop it drying out.
7 Roll out the remaining quarter to form your lid. Place it on top and trim off the excess edge.
8 Put the plastic lid on the bowl, place in a large pan with a lid big enough to hold it, and fill with water until it comes halfway up the side of the basin. Put the lid on the pan and simmer for about 3 hours. You might need to top up the water midway through.
9 After 3 hours remove (careful, it'll be hot), and leave to stand for 5 minutes before taking off the pudding basin lid.
10 Probably best served with a nice cider!

Lamb bomb

This is my version of a dish I first saw at the Jugged Hare public house on Chiswell Street, London. It's basically a delicious lamb stew wrapped in a ball of pastry with a sprig of rosemary in the top, which they set on fire like a fuse. The effect is like one of those round cartoon bombs that Wile E. Coyote might hurl at Road Runner.

INGREDIENTS

For the filling
- 1 shoulder of lamb
- 2 tablespoons of vegetable oil
- 1 sprig of rosemary
- 1 head of garlic
- 100ml of white wine

For the pastry
- 200g plain flour
- 50g butter
- 50g lard
- A pinch of salt
- A few drops of water
- 1 beaten egg to brush

Of course, you don't have to use lamb – slow-cooked pulled pork would work just as well, as indeed would jugged hare.

METHOD

1 Preheat oven to 140°C.

2 Heat the oil in a large ovenproof metal tray on the hob, add the lamb and brown all over. Add the herbs and pour the wine over.

3 Seal the tray tightly with two coats of foil and place in the oven for six hours or, even better, overnight.

4 When the lamb is cooked, cool enough to handle and falling off the bone, pick the meat off, ensuring each piece is roughly bite-sized, and discard the bones. The cooking liquid can be reduced in a pan to make the gravy.

5 To make the bomb shape you need a small, round, high-sided bowl to use as a mould. You're not after something the size of a football here, more like a child's ball. Roll out your pastry and gently line the inside of the bowl. Add the cool meat filling, gather the ends of the pastry together and crimp.

6 Place in the fridge to set again.

7 When you're ready to cook it turn it out into a baking tray so that what was the bottom is now the top. Brush with beaten egg and bake in a hot oven (180°C) for 30–40 minutes until golden brown.

8 Place a sprig of rosemary in the top and set it alight just before you take it to table. Serve with mashed potato and some greens.

Lamb shank pie

Ahh, the lamb shank, once cheap as chips. Then in the late '90s chefs and food writers starting gussying them up in red wine and serving them on beds of polenta and before you knew it they started to cost a fortune. Still, if you can get them, do so, as they're really tasty.

INGREDIENTS

For the filling
- 4 lamb shanks
- 2 diced carrots
- 2 diced medium onions
- 1 small diced floury potato (optional)
- 1 diced stick of celery
- 3 cloves of chopped garlic
- Teaspoon of tomato purée
- 500ml of stock
- Glass of white wine
- Tablespoon of flour
- 2 tinned anchovy fillets or a teaspoon of anchovy sauce
- Salt and pepper
- Vegetable oil

For the pastry
- 300g of shortcrust pastry (see page 32)
- Greaseproof paper, tin foil

This pie calls for the bones of each shank to be protruding up through the pastry crust. Serves four (one shank each).

FRENCH TRIMMING

If you get your shanks from the butcher and he's not busy, ask him to French-trim them. What you want is the top 3cm trimmed off the pointed end of the shank. Make sure he gives you the trimming too.

If you're doing it at home, it's not that hard. Run a small sharp knife around the meat and gradually cut into the flesh. Remove and save the offcuts. Scrape down the bone with the knife to ensure it's as clean as possible and free from any meat bits.

THE DISH

Think carefully about which dish you're going to serve this pie in. You need a tall, high-sided one that can hold the shanks snugly together. You know your pots and pans best, you decide.

A CARTOUCHE

Like most pies, you're aiming to make a stew first, or in this case a braise. You'll also need what chefs call a cartouche. This is a piece of greaseproof paper that you put over stews to stop them drying out and colouring on top while still allowing the sauce to reduce, unlike, say, using a casserole lid.

To make one lay out a sheet of greaseproof paper, turn your casserole dish upside down and place it on the paper. With a pencil or sharp knife, score around the pot. Remove and then cut out the resulting circle. It should be roughly the same size. Also cut out four pieces of tin foil about 10cm square.

METHOD

1 Peel and chop all the vegetables and French-trim the shanks, if your butcher didn't do them.
2 Heat the oil in a casserole on the hob. Dust the shanks in seasoned flour, brown each one in the casserole on a high heat and set aside.
3 Then brown the trimmed bits from the top of the shank (waste not want not).
4 Turn down the heat, add a bit more oil and tip in the vegetables.
5 Once they've begun to soften and take on a little colour, add the flour.
6 Then add the wine, anchovies and stock.
7 Place the shanks back in the casserole with their bones sticking up.
8 You want to sort of wedge them together supported by the vegetables, yet submerged in the liquid.
9 Now, place your cartouche over the ingredients. You'll need to cut four little holes that match where your bones stick out. Wrap the tin foil around the bones – this is to stop them taking on too much colour in the oven. You don't have to do this, but the finished pie will look nicer. Also, burned bone doesn't taste very nice.
10 Phew. After all that, pop it in the oven at 140°C for 3 hours and go and have a well-earned rest.
11 After about 3 hours the shanks should be cooked. Remove from the oven and leave somewhere to cool. Gently remove the foil and cartouche. You can, of course, do all this the day before you want your pie.
12 You know that high-sided dish you had in mind? Now's the time to use it. Don't worry if your meat is falling off the bone. In fact, if you want you can remove and shred it. Place the filling in the dish, with the bones pointing upward.
13 Roll out the chilled pastry and place over the dish. Poke the bones through the pastry, and trim off any excess. Brush with egg or milk.
14 Place the pie in a hot oven (180°C) for about 30 minutes until the pastry is golden and the filling heated through.

Mince lamb filo pie

A North African-inspired pie this, so think lamb, dates, pine nuts and paper-thin sheets of filo pastry. You can tweak the spicing depending on your palate. It's interesting that the combination of meat, fruit and spice is very similar to the Dartmouth pie (page 77), yet we think of that as medieval, whereas this feels almost contemporary.

INGREDIENTS

For the filling
- 500g lamb mince
- 1 medium onion diced
- 80ml of water or stock
- 1 teaspoon of harissa paste
- 1 teaspoon of cinnamon
- 1 teaspoon of mixed spice
- ½ teaspoon of ground cumin
- 1 tablespoon of oil
- Handful of dried apricots
- Handful of pine nuts
- Chopped parsley

For the pastry
- 1 pack of filo pastry
- 50g melted butter

METHOD

1 First toast the pine nuts over a low heat in a dry frying pan and set aside.

2 In the same pan, add the oil then fry the onion and lamb mince. When done, add the harissa and other spices. Add the stock or water and simmer gently for about 15 minutes.

3 Add the apricots and toasted pine nuts, as well as the parsley, and leave to cool.

4 Melt the butter in a microwave or saucepan and have it ready on standby along with a pastry brush. You have to work quickly with filo, as you don't want it to dry out.

5 Brush one sheet of filo with the melted butter and place in a shallow ovenproof pie dish. You want the edges to hang over the lip of the dish. Brush another sheet and place the other way, and repeat a third time.

6 Add the meat filling, and smooth down.

7 Fold the overhanging edges of the filo into the centre, and brush again with the melted butter. If it needs it, add one more well-buttered sheet of filo on top.

8 Press down gently, then bake in a preheated oven (180°C) for 20 minutes until golden brown.

9 Best served warm rather than hot. Minty yoghurt and some mixed leaves are the only extras it needs.

Pork and leek pie

Pork, leek and mustard are all flavours that play well together, and this pie features all of them. Leeks are members of the onion family – they're basically spring onion's older cousin who's let himself go a bit.

INGREDIENTS

For the filling (large pie tin)

- 2 tablespoons of vegetable oil
- 450g pork steaks cut into chunks
- 1 small onion, diced
- 2 leeks, sliced
- 1 teaspoon of thyme leaves
- 150ml of chicken stock (or pork stock if you've got it)
- 1 teaspoon of cornflour, mixed with water
- 1 teaspoon of Dijon or wholegrain mustard (or English if you like it hot)
- 2 tablespoons of crème fraîche
- 200ml cider
- Salt and pepper

For the pastry

I've gone for shortcrust (see page 32). For a large tin you'll need 250g for a single crust, and another 350g for a double crust pie (total 600g).

- 1 egg, beaten, to glaze

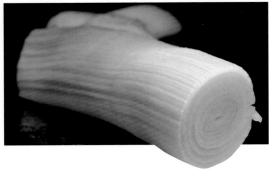

A word on preparing the leeks. Now, you *can* just chop them into discs, nothing wrong with that per se. But if you want to look a little more refined, cut each leek into 2in (5cm) rods, then cut in half again lengthways. Put the flat side on the board and cut lengthways again. What you end up with is lots of very thin, 2in-long ribbons. Leeks need very little cooking, so add them last to preserve a little of that green punchiness.

This recipe will serve four.

METHOD

1. Peel and chop the onion and prepare the leeks. Heat the oil in a casserole and brown the pork meat. Remove and set aside.
2. Turn down the heat and add the onion – cook until soft. Add the meat back in, then add the stock, cider, thyme, mustard, crème fraîche, cornflour dissolved in a little water, and season well.
3. Simmer for 25 minutes until sauce has reduced and thickened. Leave to cool.
4. Roll out the pastry and line your pie tin. Spoon the cooled filling in and, if using, add a pie bird (page 20).
5. Coat the rim with egg wash and place the lid on. Crimp the edge to seal it and brush the top with the egg wash.
6. Place in a preheated oven (200°C) and bake for around 30 minutes until pastry is golden brown.

Mutton pot pie

If you're in London's West End and looking for somewhere to sit down, have a beer and enjoy a good pie, then you can do *a lot* worse than the Ape and Bird public house on Shaftsbury Avenue. This recipe is the sort of good cooking you'll get there from head chef Alex Windebank.

Recipe serves eight to ten.

INGREDIENTS

For the filling

- 1 leg of mutton (1.5–2kg)
- 1 bottle of red wine
- 1 litre of chicken stock
- 2 bay leaves
- Large sprig of thyme
- Large sprig of rosemary
- 1 bulb of garlic split in half
- 3 carrots diced
- 4 sticks of celery diced
- 2 large onions diced
- 4 cloves of garlic minced
- 2 tablespoons of English mustard
- 2 tablespoons of Worcestershire sauce

For the suet pastry

- 375g self-raising flour
- 2 teaspoons of salt
- 120g butter (cold and cubed)
- 200g suet
- 250ml water

METHOD

1 Preheat the oven to 150°C.

2 Colour the mutton leg in a hot pan, place in a deep casserole dish, add the bay leaves, herbs and garlic and cover with both the wine and chicken stock. Place in the oven for 6 hours.

3 While that's cooking, make the pastry. In a bowl, rub the flour, salt and butter with your fingertips until forming breadcrumbs. Add the suet and the water. Combine, and roll out to 3mm thickness.

4 Remove the lamb from the oven and allow to sit for 1 hour to cool.

5 Sweat the diced veg and garlic over a medium heat for about 20 minutes or until soft.

6 Remove the lamb from the liquid and pass the liquid through a sieve into the same pan as the cooking veg. Bring to the boil and allow to simmer until reduced by two-thirds.

7 Whilst reducing, strip the lamb off the bone and shred into small pieces. Once reduced mix the meat into the liquid and add the mustard, Worcestershire sauce and season to taste.

8 Place the mix in a pie dish (or pie dishes) and cover with the suet pastry. Egg wash the pastry and place in a preheated oven at 190°C for about 20 minutes or until golden brown and piping hot throughout.

Chilli beef pie

Ah, chilli. It conjures up images of life under the stars after a long day driving cattle across the south-western US. Yet in the UK it usually comes on a baked potato with a bit of salad. You've got to laugh at the way us Brits 'do' other cultures' food. But then, what *does* constitute authentic these days? The International Chili Society based in the USA organise a cook-off every year, and the 2013 winning recipe featured prunes! One thing's for sure, kidney beans don't feature in a Tex-Mex-style chilli.

Chilli's effectively just a spicy meat stew, and like most slow-cooked dishes it tastes even better the next day. But sometimes you don't just want to eat more chilli and rice again, so why not use it as a filling in a pie?

INGREDIENTS

This is my basic chilli con carne recipe, though I do often add or subtract things depending on what's in my fridge. Feel free to use your own recipe.

For the filling
- 1 tablespoon of vegetable oil
- 1kg minced beef
- 2 onions chopped
- 1 red pepper chopped
- 4 cloves of garlic peeled and chopped
- 4 chillies, finely chopped (chipotle are smoked, dried jalapeño and lend a smoky flavour)
- 1 teaspoon of chilli powder
- 1 teaspoon of ground cumin
- ½ teaspoon of smoked paprika
- ½ teaspoon of cinnamon
- ½ teaspoon of dried oregano
- ½ teaspoon of dried marjoram
- ½ can of plum tomatoes, blitzed (or passata)
- 500ml of beef stock
- 1 can of kidney beans (optional)

For the pastry
- 600g of shortcrust pastry. Each double-crust pie will need approx 300g – 150g for the base and a smidge less for the lid.
- 1 egg to glaze
- A pinch of paprika or chilli powder

METHOD

Make the filling the day before you make the pastry.

To make the filling
1. In a large pot, add a little of the oil and brown the mince in small batches and remove. Add the onion and the pepper, and cook until soft. Return the mince again, the dried spices and herbs and the fresh chillies. Add the tomatoes, stock and beans if using.
2. Bring up to a simmer then pop into a low oven (around 120°C) for at least 2 hours or longer. Stir it after one hour and check on it after two.
3. This should give you enough filling for two portions of chilli on day one, and still leave enough left over to make two small individual double-crust pies. Of course, you could choose not to eat the chilli on day one and use it to fill a large tin.

To make the pastry
4. Make the pastry (see page 32). Cut it into 4x150g pieces.
5. Roll out two pieces for your pie base and line each small pie tin. Roll out your two lids and set aside.
6. Add the cold, leftover chilli filling.
7. Brush the rim with egg or milk, attach your lid and make a small hole in the top.
8. Brush the lid with egg wash, and as a final flourish sprinkle a pinch of chilli powder over it.
9. Serve with some hot chilli sauce and freshly made guacamole (or jacket potato and salad).

Pork with fennel and cider pot pie

Pork and apples are a happy marriage, but this recipe introduces fennel like some flavoursome femme fatale. Fennel bulbs are very firm, consequently they need long, slow cooking to break them down. Thankfully the same goes for pork cheeks, hence why I've used them here.

INGREDIENTS

For the filling
- A glug of vegetable oil
- 6 pork cheeks chopped into chunks
- 50g of seasoned flour for dusting the pork
- 2 fennel bulbs finely sliced
- 1 medium onion
- 200ml of chicken stock
- 200ml of dry cider
- 2 tablespoons of crème fraîche
- 1 tablespoon of Pernod
- Small handful of parsley chopped (or if you really want to up the aniseed flavour, use tarragon)
- 1 teaspoon of Dijon mustard
- Salt and pepper

For the pastry
- 250g of pastry (puff, rough puff or flaky)
- 1 beaten egg

This recipe will serve four. You can make four individual pies or a larger single- or double-crust pie – the choice, as ever, is yours. Though I love a double-crust, I do think there are some fillings that work better as single-crust pot pies, and this is perhaps one of them. It's also one for the lighter pastries (see page 19). You'll need 250g for a single-topped pie.

METHOD

To make the filling
1 Slice the onion and then the fennel, add the oil to a frying pan (with a lid if possible) and, on a low heat, gently fry them both, keeping them moving from time to time.
2 Chop the pork and dust with seasoned flour (see page 60).
3 After 20 minutes the fennel should have started to soften and caramelise. Remove it and set aside.
4 Wipe out the pan, add a glug more oil and turn up the heat a bit. Add the pork and colour a little.
5 Return the fennel. Add the Pernod, stock, cider, mustard, crème fraîche and seasoning, and place in a low oven (140°C) for at least two hours until the cheeks are cooked through and falling apart and the sauce has thickened. Add the parsley last of all to retain the colour and leave to cool.

You could serve this filling as a stew, with rice or mashed potatoes, but this is the *Men's Pie Manual*, so we're going to break out the pastry, as you'd expect.

To make the pastry
6 Preheat the oven to 200°C, beat your egg.
7 Spoon the cooled filling into a shallow dish. Rub a knob of butter around the edge and add a pie bird in the centre.
8 Unroll your cold puff pastry over the dish, poking through the head of the bird, and crimp down on to the dish's edge.
9 Brush quickly with the beaten egg and get into the hot oven (200°C) for 20 minutes until the pastry is puffed up and golden brown.

Dartmouth pie

A curious pie, and perhaps the last of the medieval style of pie, which sees the filling made with meat combined with sweet things like dried fruit and lots of sugar. Mince pies were once like this too, though they lost their meat filling sometime in the late Victorian era. I doubt you'll see a Dartmouth pie on a menu in Devon these days, or anywhere else for that matter, but I've included it more for historical purposes.

One or two modern recipes call for pork, but actually mutton is the traditional meat used. Don't use lamb mince, however – it just won't have the flavour. The recipe from 1822 in *A Modern System of Domestic Cookery, or, The Housekeeper's Guide*, by M. Radcliffe, also calls for a sort of hot-water crust pastry casing, but I've opted for shortcrust here. As for the size, I've gone for small round-shaped pies, but you could make a large single one.

I've also added some more Middle Eastern spices and dialled down the sugar element by replacing it with honey. But as ever, tweak as you see fit.

This recipe will serve four.

INGREDIENTS

For the filling

- 500g mutton mince
- 1 medium onion finely chopped
- 50g mixed dried fruits (currants, sultanas)
- ½ teaspoon of sumac (a mixed spice from the Middle East – optional)
- Handful of dried apricots
- Handful of dried prunes
- Zest of an orange
- ½ teaspoon of cinnamon
- ½ teaspoon of ginger
- ½ teaspoon of allspice
- ½ teaspoon of crushed juniper berries
- ½ teaspoon of freshly grated nutmeg
- Tablespoon of honey
- 50ml of stock
- Salt and plenty of pepper (another medieval 'luxury')

For the pastry

- Enough for four double-crust pies made in small, round pie tins

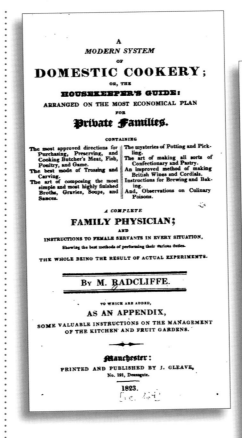

METHOD

1 Get all your ingredients ready. Fry the mince and the onion in a pan until browned.

2 Add the honey, spices, orange zest, dried fruits, apricots and prunes. Pour over the stock and let it simmer for 20 minutes or so until it's all well combined. Leave to cool.

3 Remove a third of your pastry for your lids. Roll out the remainder into a square on a floured surface. Cut to roughly the right size to line your tins. Add the cooled filling, brush the rim with egg wash or milk and place the lid on. Crimp the edge with a fork.

4 Bake in a preheated oven (180°C) for around 20 minutes until the pastry is golden.

5 Allow to cool, then go all medieval on them.

Humble pie

In the 14th century 'numbles' was the name given to the internal organs of an animal, predominantly deer (today the word used to describe the process of removal is 'gralloching'). These bits were often used in pies. Indeed, Samuel Pepys does just that on 5 July 1662: 'I having some venison given me a day or two ago, and so I had a shoulder roasted, another baked, and the umbles baked in a pie, and all very well done.'

Meanwhile, across town, so to speak, the word humble meaning 'having or showing a modest or low importance or rank' arrived in our language from the Latin *humilis*, 'low, lowly'. Then, somewhere in history, things got mixed up and we now have the saying 'to eat humble pie'. You might have read elsewhere that the poor were given the bits of an animal that weren't valued, so you can see why the confusion of 'numble' and 'humble' probably came about. However, although today we think of offal as the lowly bits of an animal, in times past they would have been highly prized. Pepys, for instance, didn't give away these important ingredients, he kept and ate them.

Pepys may have even followed this recipe in *The Accomplisht Cook* by Robert May (1660): 'To make Umble-Pies. Lay minced beef-suet in the bottom of the pie, or slices of interlarded bacon, and the umbles cut as big as small dice, with some bacon cut in the same form, and seasoned with nutmeg, pepper, and salt, fill your pies with it, and slices of bacon and butter, close it up and bake it, and liquor it with claret, butter, and stripped thyme.'

Today getting your hands on fresh deer offal is a little tricky, so my version uses lamb's liver – which is one of the cheapest bits of meat you can get – and a dash of sherry, which isn't very cheap but, I think, is worth it. But leave it out if you like.

INGREDIENTS

For the filling (enough for a medium-sized pie tin)

- 50g butter
- 2 medium onions chopped
- 600g lamb's liver sliced thinly
- 50g pancetta or smoked bacon diced
- 25g plain flour seasoned
- 1 teaspoon of chopped thyme leaves
- 50ml Oloroso sherry (not very humble)
- 200ml beef stock
- 1 teaspoon of cornflour
- Salt and pepper

For the pastry

Shortcrust pastry (page 32) works best here, either double- or single-crust (though you could conceivably use hot-water crust). This recipe should make enough filling for a medium-sized pie dish.

METHOD

To make the filling

1 Melt the butter in a frying pan, add the bacon and onions and fry gently until translucent and soft. Remove.
2 Dust the liver with seasoned flour, turn up the heat and fry the liver for a matter of moments – you don't want to overcook it, just give it a tiny bit of colour on the outside.
3 Add the bacon and onion back to the pan and cook until soft.
4 Fling in the sherry and cook off the alcohol, then add the beef stock and thyme and simmer until the sauce has reduced.
5 Mix the cornflour with 5ml of cold water and add to the sauce to thicken slightly.
6 Turn out the heat and return the liver to the pan and leave to cool.

To make the pastry

7 Make (see page 32) or buy shortcrust pastry.
8 If making a double-crust pie, cut your pastry into a 150g piece for the lid, and a 200g piece for the base.
9 Roll out the base and line your tin with the pastry. Trim off the excess and add the filling to the centre.
10 Brush the lip with milk or beaten egg, and roll the lid on top.
11 Crimp down the edge and wash the top with more beaten egg.
12 Place in a hot oven (200°C) for 25 minutes until the pastry is golden brown and cooked through.
13 Remove and leave to cool a little before taking the pie out of the tin and putting it on a wire rack.

Serve with plenty of wine, which is what Pepys would have done, followed by wenching at a playhouse in Southwark.

Fry-up pie

According to Seb Emina, author of *The Breakfast Bible*, there must be nine items on the plate to constitute a full English: eggs, bacon, sausage, mushrooms, tomatoes, black pudding, toast, baked beans and some form of potato.

Now, whilst you technically *could* put all those things in a pie casing, I think it might just be overdoing it. So instead I've settled for what I consider the solid midfield of a fry-up – eggs, sausage, bacon and black pudding. Beans, tomatoes and potato products are 'sides' in my opinion.

This recipe serves two people and is best made as individual pies, but you can up the ingredients to make a larger one if you prefer.

INGREDIENTS

For the filling

- 4 rashers of streaky bacon
- 4 sausages, skins removed and broken into pieces
- 2 medium eggs
- 2 'hockey pucks' of black pudding

For the pastry

- Enough shortcrust pastry for a double-crust medium pie dish, around 350g should do it (see page 32).

METHOD

1 Dice the bacon into pieces and fry in a frying pan until cooked. Remove to a side plate; then add the sausage meat, cook and remove; and finally add the black pudding, cook and remove.

2 Remove a third of your pastry for the lid and roll out the remainder on a floured surface. Line your tins and two-thirds fill with the meat mixture.

3 Make a small well in the centre of the filling. Crack an egg into a teacup or on to a saucer and gently pour into the depression at the centre of the filling. You kind of want the white to run in between the other ingredients to bind it, while the yolk stays in the centre.

4 Roll out your lid piece.

5 Brush the rim with milk or another egg well beaten, and pop the lid on. Crimp and trim the edge, and make a small hole in the top of the lid to let out any steam.

6 Bake in a preheated oven (180°C) for about 20 minutes until the pastry is golden. Serve with beans, hash browns, tomatoes, mushrooms (toast would be overkill surely?) and wash down with a pint of tea. Champion!

Oxtail and beef cheek pie

First top and tail your cow, as this pie uses the tasty bits that book-end the beast. Ever wondered how much masticating a cow does in its life? The answer is a lot, consequently its cheeks are some of its hardest-working muscles. The tail, at the other end, is also constantly moving.

Hard work gives you flavour, but you too have to work to get it out; marinating helps. The tougher muscles need much longer, slower, lower cooking than the likes of the fillet, which, running down the centre of the spine, does bugger all work and consequently can be pretty much cooked with a cigarette lighter.

The prunes and the redcurrant jelly add a sweetness to the filling, but they're optional.

This recipe serves six.

INGREDIENTS

For the filling

- 6 ox cheeks
- 3 or 4 bits of oxtail
- 2 medium onions diced
- 2 peeled carrots chopped into big chunks
- 1 stick of celery diced
- 1 bottle of ale (a dark flavourful one like porter or stout)
- 200ml of beef stock
- ½ teaspoon of thyme leaves
- 1 teaspoon of Worcestershire sauce
- A few dried prunes
- 1 tablespoon of redcurrant jelly
- Oil for frying (beef dripping is even better, if you've got some)
- 40g of seasoned flour

For the pastry

- You'll need 600g of shortcrust pastry for this (see page 32). Why not gild the lily and enrich it with suet or egg yolks?

METHOD

1 Cut each cheek in two, then put with the oxtail in a large bowl and pour the beer over it. Leave to marinate in the fridge overnight. Make the pastry and chill in the fridge.

2 Remove the meat and save the marinade. Pat dry with kitchen towel and dust in seasoned flour.

3 Heat the oil in a casserole and brown the oxtail and cheeks. Remove and set aside.

4 In the same pan, gently cook the onion, carrot and celery until softened and translucent.

5 Add the meat back to the pan, add the beer and the stock to cover it. Add the thyme, prunes, redcurrant jelly and Worcestershire sauce.

6 Pop a circle of greaseproof paper (a cartouche) over the surface and place in a preheated oven (140°C) for 2½ hours until the meat is tender.

7 Remove from the oven and lift out the oxtail pieces and set aside to cool. Flake off any meat that's still stuck to the bones, and return it to the pan. Discard the bones, their work is done. Leave the pie filling to cool. All of this can be done in advance, and as usual the mixture can be frozen at this stage into portions.

8 Cut off a third of your pastry for the lid and roll out the remainder on a floured surface. Line your pie tin and add the cold filling. If your pie dish is quite large you may want to use a pie funnel.

9 Brush egg wash around the edge. Roll out the lid and place on top. Trim and crimp the edge and brush the lid with more egg wash.

10 Cook in a preheated oven at 180°C for around 25 minutes until the pastry is golden.

Espresso cup pies

Teeny-tiny starter pies, great for using up any leftover filling, as well as trimmings of pastry. Just don't call them 'canapies', you'll sound silly.

INGREDIENTS
- 4/6 espresso cups (make sure they're ovenproof, or use at your own risk!)
- 100g of pie filling
- 200g of puff pastry

You can pretty much use any pie filling from within this book. The key thing to remember is to ensure that any meat or vegetables are chopped down smaller – no one wants a huge chuck of beef in a small cup! Rather it should be smaller morsels, and have plenty of sauce, more like a stew, or even a chunky soup, as people are liable to lift the cup to their lips.

METHOD
1 Spoon some of the filling into the espresso cups so it comes almost up to the lip, and lay a square of puff pastry over the top. Don't bother trimming or crimping it, just let it fall down the sides naturally. Brush with a little melted butter.
2 Prick a hole in the top with a cocktail stick and put into a hot oven (200°C). They'll take 10 minutes at most, probably less. Remove when the pastry is puffed up and golden.

A more coffee-focused filling

Make the beef and ale pie filling from page 63, but try using Meantime Brewery's coffee porter. This beer was the first to be given Fair Trade certification, as they use coffee from a co-operative in Rwanda. It'll be subtle, but you should get some of that coffee-like flavour and bitterness coming through.

You can make this in cups that are larger. Retro enamelled cups would work. I wouldn't use fine bone china, however.

3 Allow to cool for 5 minutes, then serve on a saucer with a teaspoon. Who says pies can't be sophisticated?

Meatball pie

You've a couple of different options with this pie, depending on how much effort you're able to put in and who you're making it for. You can either make your meatballs from scratch, use pre-made ones and cook them or, if you're really lazy and like the taste of mystery meat, use a tin of pre-made, pre-cooked meatballs. But if you're going to be that lazy, you might as well buy a pre-made pie.

INGREDIENTS

- 1 pack of 12 meatballs
- 1 red pepper finely diced
- 1 onion finely chopped
- 2 cloves of garlic, crushed
- 1 tin of good-quality tomato-based pasta sauce
- 1 pack of pre-made pastry
- Tablespoon of vegetable oil
- Handful of grated cheese
- 1 egg to brush

So, let's assume you're going for the pre-made but raw meatballs you can find in the supermarket meat aisle these days – after all there's some rather good ones out there.

For the sauce, you *can* fry chopped onion and garlic, before adding a can of chopped tomatoes, salt and pepper and oregano. Or just buy a jar of pasta sauce.

For the pastry, it's a similar story. Yes, you can make it from scratch, or just use ready-made. I'd favour the latter. This is one of those 'shortcut' easy family-friendly pies you just put together in less than 30 minutes.

METHOD

1 Chop the onion and pepper and fry in the oil until soft and translucent. Remove, and add the meatballs, gently swilling the pan round so they roll and colour all over. Add the garlic and the cooked onion and pepper and cook until the garlic's done.

2 Pour the jar of sauce over it and let it all simmer for 10 minutes on a low heat until the sauce has thickened. You don't want it too runny. Leave to cool.

3 Preheat your oven to 180°C. Unroll your sheet of pastry and cut into a large circle. Put this on a 10cm round baking tray.

4 Add the filling, making sure it's piled up in the centre, then sprinkle the top with the grated cheese. Fold the edges up and over the filling, leaving a large hole in the centre.

5 Brush the outside with beaten egg.

6 Place in the oven and bake for 30 minutes until pie is golden brown.

7 Serve with something green – broccoli, perhaps, or green beans.

Melton Mowbray pork pie

The rural market town of Melton Mowbray in Leicestershire lends its name to one of Britain's best-known, best-loved and just downright best pies. A Melton Mowbray pork pie could easily lay claim to being the king of British pies, and in 2008 it was the first pie to achieve PGI status, meaning it has to be made a certain way, with certain ingredients, in a defined geographical region.

INGREDIENTS

For the hot-water crust pastry

- 120g plain flour
- 60g lard
- 2.5g of salt
- 35ml of water
- Beaten egg to glaze

For the filling

- 225g lean pork, chopped (shoulder would be ideal, but not bacon or ham)
- Salt and pepper
- 125ml pork stock and 15g gelatine

Indeed, you might say the town is the pie capital of Britain, as it also plays host to the annual British Pie Awards (see page 180). As if that wasn't enough the region is also 'home' to Stilton cheese-making (the history of Stilton is a fascinating one). There's some cracking beers brewed nearby to wash it all down too. In short, you should pay the town a visit, and buy a pork pie. But if you can't wait that long, here's how to make one.

This recipe has been kindly provided by Dickinson & Morris, who are the oldest pork pie bakery and last remaining producer of genuine Melton Mowbray pork pies in Melton itself. They first served up pies in 1851. The recipe will make a 450g (1lb) pork pie.

METHOD

To make the pastry

1 Sift flour and salt into a warm bowl and rub in 15g of lard.
2 Gently heat the remaining lard and water together until boiling, then add to the flour, mixing until mixture is cool enough to knead. Knead well to ensure no air is in the pastry. Keep aside a quarter of the pastry for the lid.
3 Make the remaining piece of pastry into a ball and leave in the fridge overnight.

To make the filling

4 Dice the fresh uncured pork into small pieces and season well with salt and pepper.
5 Make the jelly at a later stage, whilst baking, by dissolving the gelatine in pork stock.

To make the pie the right shape

A key part of a Melton Mowbray pork pie is its distinctive shape, and the fact that it's not baked in a tin but is 'hand-raised':

6 Remove the pastry from the fridge at least 2–3 hours before making the pie case. Begin by gently squeezing/tempering the pastry ball between your hands so that it becomes pliable and mouldable. Loosely form into a flattened ball. (Tip: take great care not to overwork the pastry.)

7 Using a floured surface, circle the pastry between your hands to begin bringing the wall sides up.

8 Take your dolly – or, if you don't have one, a regular-sized jam jar – and push firmly into the centre of the pastry. This should raise the wall sides up and outwards, ready for shaping.

9 Whilst rotating the dolly in a circular motion, squeeze the pastry with your hands and at the same time work the pastry up and around the body of the dolly. The pastry should have a regular and even thickness all the way round. (Tip: make sure you don't push the dolly through the bottom of the pastry case!)

10 Raise the pastry to the top of the dolly and prepare to remove the dolly from the pastry case.

11 Gently remove the pastry case from the dolly by teasing the pastry away from the sides with your thumbs. Slowly remove the dolly from the case.

12 Firmly place your ball of coarsely chopped, seasoned, fresh pork into the pastry case, moulding the sides to the meat to ensure no air remains in the body of the pie.

13 Dampen the inside rim of the pastry case with egg. Roll out the reserved pastry to an even thickness and cut out a circular lid. Place on top of the meat and pastry case.

14 Seal and finish the pie by hand, gently pinching the lid and wall sides together. It's very important to ensure the lid is very securely sealed to the pastry case, otherwise the sides will collapse during baking.

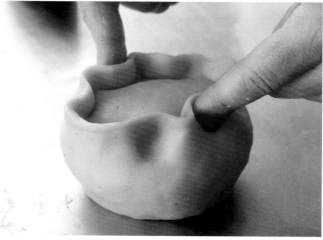

15 At opposite points around the circumference of the pie push the sides in to create a crimped finish to the top of the pie.

16 Chill the pie for at least 1 hour in a fridge, or for best results overnight.

17 Your pie will now be ready to be placed in the oven! Just lightly brush the top of the pie (not the crimp) with egg and make a hole in the lid centre. Place on a baking tray, and bake in the traditional way – without a supporting hoop – to give a distinctive bow-sided shape to the walls. Bake in the oven at Gas Mark 4 (220°C) for approximately 1¼ to 1½ hours (times will vary according to oven type and make).

18 Once baked until a rich, golden brown, cool the pie, make two holes in the lid and pour in the jelly. Leave to cool further, ideally overnight, in a fridge.

Remember, a pork pie is designed to be eaten cold, not reheated. To enjoy the pie at its best, remove from the fridge at least an hour before consuming.

Fidget pie

Everyone knows pork and apple is a winning combination, and in the county of Shropshire they go one better by using both these ingredients in a pie. Cheese and cider often join the party too. All of these things are found in abundance in the region, yet the pie itself was in danger of dying out just a few years ago. Thankfully a resurgent food scene centred on Ludlow has helped bring it back from the brink.

Ones you might see in the shops and delis in the town often have a pastry bottom but a mashed potato topping, though I've seen other varieties further afield topped with stuffing. Other recipes combine the potato in the filling and top with pastry, but I've gone for the spud-topped version.

The following recipe makes four individual pies.

INGREDIENTS

For the filling

- 3/4 gammon steaks
- 1 large Bramley apple peeled
- 2 medium onions chopped
- 4 potatoes (mashers such as Maris Piper) peeled
- Pinch of brown sugar
- Salt and pepper
- 150ml of cider
- 100g of grated cheese
- 1 teaspoon of dried sage or a few fresh sage leaves chopped
- Tablespoon of oil
- 20g butter
- 10ml milk

For the pastry

- Shortcrust (page 32) is the best pastry to use for the pie case. If you're making 4 individual pies in small to medium-sized tins, you'll need approximately 150g of pastry for each pie (600g in total). See page 19 for pastry amounts and sizes.

METHOD

1 Make the shortcrust pastry (page 32), and when done chill it in the fridge.
2 Prepare the rest of your ingredients. Chop the onion, peel the apples and potatoes and chop into chunks, then dice the meat into strips.
3 Bring a pan of salted water to the boil and add the potatoes.
4 Heat the oil in a frying pan and add the pork slices to colour. Remove, turn down the heat, and add 10g of the butter and cook the onion and apple pieces until tender. Put the meat back in and add the cider, sage and sugar and season well. Simmer until the cider has reduced and the apples mushed down. Leave to cool.
5 Drain and mash the potatoes, add the rest of the butter and the milk. Leave to cool.
6 Grate the cheese and preheat your oven to 180°C.
7 Lightly butter your pastry tins.
8 Cut the pastry into four equal-sized amounts and roll out flat. Cut to fit your tins. Trim the excess.
9 Spoon the filling into the pastry case. Scatter the grated cheese over it.
10 Spread (or pipe, if you've got a piping bag) the cooled mashed potato over the top of the filling, ensuring it covers it and meets the pastry edge.
11 Run the tines of a fork over to create a pattern if you want to.
12 Bake in the oven for about 25 minutes until the pastry is cooked and the mash is golden. Leave to cool.

Gala pie

Ah gala pie, a pork pie (see page 84) with a secret hidden extra; a hard-boiled egg at its centre. Like a pork pie, it takes a bit of time to make, but the results are well worth it. Unveil a home-made gala pie and you'll be king of the picnic rug for sure, while other men hold their manhoods cheap.

INGREDIENTS

For the hot water crust pastry
- 225g plain flour
- 225g strong flour
- 150g lard
- 125ml of boiling water
- 1 teaspoon of salt
- 1 teaspoon of sugar

For the filling
- 1 hard boiled egg
- 250g of minced pork
- 50g finely chopped smoked bacon or lardons
- 1 teaspoon of chopped sage
- 1 pinch of freshly-grated nutmeg.
- Salt and pepper

Traditionally these pies are square or more often oblong shaped. However there's no reason why you can't make a round one. I've opted for individual ones here, (ok, could maybe be shared between two) in small but tall pork pie tins, but you could always up the quantities and make a large 8in (20cm) one to share. Also you're more likely to have a round high-sided cake tin with a removable bottom rather than a oblong loaf tin with one.

For this pie I'm leaving out the jelly, but if you're a big jelly fan and have got time, just reduce the pork filling amount by 20g and follow the jelly stock making process on page 51.

Finally just a word on the egg. Unlike a Scotch egg, where a runny centre is rather nice, you want these eggs boiled solid. The key to boiling an egg well isn't so much of rapid bolding, but more of a rolling gentle boil. You'll need to give these ten minutes at least from a cold start.

This version feeds one hungry fella, or two. Serve with an apple, chunk of cheese, a gherkin, and glass of beer.

METHOD

Make the filling
1 First prepare the meat. Finely chop the bacon as much as you can, and set aside. Get the pork mince out of the packet and ready. Finely chop the sage and grate the nutmeg and combine all together along with a good pinch of salt and pepper.
2 Next boil the egg. From a cold water start, 8–10 minutes should do. Then plunge into cold water. When cool, remove the shell and reserve.

Make the pasty
3 Melt the lard gently in a pan, but do not let it boil. Combine the flour and salt in a bowl. Add the water to the melted lard first, then add this mix to the flour. Mix together with a knife. When cool enough to handle bring together with your fingers and kneed a little.
4 Reserve a quarter of the dough for the lid. Working quickly before the dough sets, roll out the remaining dough bigger than your tin and gently fit it in. You want some hanging over the side.
5 Roll out the remaining quarter into a disc that fits easily over the top and reserve.
6 Half fill the lined tin with the pork meat mix, then take your egg and place in the centre of the pie. Build up the rest of the pork meat around the sides. Really stuff it in, as the meat mix will shrink a little when cooking.

7   If you're planning to add jelly, make a small trench with your finger running away from the centre of the pie to the edge. This will help guide the jelly stock down the meat centre and ensure it reaches the gap between it and the pastry case.

8   Place your lid on top of the pie and secure with egg wash. Make a small hole in the centre of the lid to let the steam and any fat out.

9   Bake in a hot oven 200°C / 180°C fan oven for 15 minutes. Turn the oven down to 150°C and bake for another 30 minutes. Remove from the oven and leave to stand until completely cold.

10 If adding jelly, remove the cool pie from the tin, warm up the jelly stock in the microwave or a pan, and transfer to a small jug. Place the funnel in the hole on the top of the pie and ever so gently add the jelly stock a bit at a time.

The never-ending egg?

When you see gala pie in the supermarkets, it always contains a slice of the middle of the egg rather than, say, just the white tip of the egg. The way commercial pie makers do this is to take separated egg white and yolk and make a long cylindrical egg using two special moulds. First the yolk is poured into a small cylinder and cooked. It's then carefully removed from the mould and placed into a bigger one where the whites are poured around it. This too is then gently cooked. When the mould is removed, the foot long 'egg' is placed in the pie on top of half the pork meat ensuring every slice contains a whole slice of egg.

CHAPTER 5
CHICKEN AND GAME PIES

Chicken is the most popular meat in the UK – nearly everyone likes chicken. When buying it you should always buy whole chickens and break them down yourself. This way you'll save money, and have bits left over for making into pies and, most importantly, stock. So you might take the breasts off for a recipe, roast the thighs separately, and make stock from the carcass. I think chicken pies taste better when made with leftover chicken anyway, so factor in pie-making as one of your Sunday evening activities. And remember, breasts for show, thighs for a pro – that, gentlemen, is where the flavour is on a chicken.

When you buy chicken, *please* buy free-range birds. They'll have had a much better life, which in turn means they're better for you. Cheap chicken is often 'tumbled' in water to add weight. A recent investigation found some frozen breasts offered for sale were almost 20% water and additives. Most chickens available are a few months old when killed, meaning they've not really developed much flavour. If you can, seek out a mature bird, and taste what your forefathers' chicken tasted like. Back then, a bird only went in the pot when it had spent a lifetime roaming around and laying eggs.

Unlike chicken, game birds aren't eaten nearly enough in this country. If you said to the average person in the street, 'Would you like some low-fat, free-range, British meat for under a fiver?' they'd probably say, 'Yes please' ... until they found out it's pheasant or rabbit. Then they'd go all squeamish and tell you how they have to be somewhere else. That isn't you, is it? You're made of sterner stuff.

Chicken and mushroom pie

An absolute classic combination (it's even a Pot Noodle flavour) that's stood the test of time. These two ingredients just work so well together. Did you know there's actually a type of large wild mushroom called 'chicken-of-the-woods' because its firm pale flesh looks like chicken breast meat when cooked?

INGREDIENTS

For the filling
- 1 tablespoon of vegetable oil
- 10g butter
- 600g cooked chicken meat (roughly half a leftover chicken)
- 300g mixed mushrooms
- 250ml of chicken stock
- 2 tablespoons of crème fraîche
- 2 cloves of garlic crushed
- 1 large onion, chopped
- 1 small glass of white wine
- 1 teaspoon of thyme leaves
- Salt and pepper
- 1 beaten egg
- 1 handful of peas

For the pastry
- I think this filling suits a puff-topped pot pie, but as ever would work equally well in a double-lined shortcrust pie.
- 500g rough puff pastry (either pre-made – you may need two packets – or see page 35).

The key with any use of mushrooms in cooking is to use a variety, that way you get a different taste, shape and texture. White button mushrooms are the pawns of the mushroom world – they're only really good for bulking-out filling. Chestnut offer a bit more flavour, on top of that you should consider a large portobello or two. Finally, break out the big guns flavour-wise by rehydrating some porcini mushrooms.

This recipe makes a large pie that will serve six.

METHOD

1. Melt the oil and the butter in a pan and gently cook the onion until soft. Add the garlic and the mushrooms and cook for about 10 minutes until they begin to soften and take on a little colour.
2. Add the stock, thyme and wine and stir.
3. Add the chicken and the crème fraîche. Leave on a low simmer for 15–20 minutes until well combined and the sauce has thickened.
4. Leave to cool. When cool, transfer to a large pie tin or dish with a pie bird in the centre. Preheat oven to 200°C.
5. Make the rough puff pastry (page 35) or roll out pre-made pastry to cover your tin (you may need two packets, depending on how big your dish is).
6. Brush the edge of the dish with egg wash, and gently unfurl the pastry from your rolling pin over the dish. Poke through the pie bird and secure.
7. Brush the surface of the pastry with the remaining egg wash until covered and place in the hot oven for 25–30 minutes until the pastry has risen and is golden brown.

Chicken and fennel pie

This recipe is from friend and fellow author Helen Graves. She was asked by Lurpak to make a pie that would feature in one of their advertising campaigns. No pressure, then! The ingredients listed will fill an 18–20cm pie dish.

INGREDIENTS

For the filling
- 1 cooked free-range chicken (I used a roast chicken but you could use cooked chicken pieces if you don't want to roast one)
- 2 bulbs of fennel, tops, bottoms and core removed and finely sliced
- ½ a large onion sliced
- 4 smoked bacon rashers diced
- 1 large leek sliced
- 3 cloves of garlic crushed
- 1 small handful of chopped parsley
- Splash of white wine
- A dollop of wholegrain mustard (optional)
- Oil, for cooking
- 350–400ml béchamel or white sauce (bought or home-made)

For the pastry
- The pastry is puff but I prefer shortcrust, so here's my recipe. Just use whichever you prefer.
- 100g butter at room temperature
- 220g plain flour (not strong white bread flour)
- A large pinch of salt
- 1 egg beaten

METHOD

1 Prepare the pastry by sieving the flour and salt into a large bowl. Cut the softened butter into cubes and add it to the bowl. Using a knife, start cutting the butter into the flour until it's fairly well mixed. You can now use your hands to start rubbing the butter into the flour – do this as lightly as possible. If you try to squidge the butter between your fingers too much the pastry will become tough.

2 When it resembles fine crumbs, get some cold water (the colder the better) and add a tablespoon at a time, cutting it in with the knife each time, until it starts to come together. When it starts to form large lumps, use your hands to bring it together into a ball. It should leave the bowl clean. Rest in the fridge for 30 minutes.

3 Heat a splash of olive oil in a pan and add the bacon to it. Once the bacon is cooked add the leeks, garlic, fennel and onion (plus the wine if using) and cook on a very low heat with the lid on for around 15 minutes.

4 Preheat your oven to 200°C.

To assemble the pie

5 Cut off a third of your pastry. This will be the lid.

6 Roll out the remaining pastry into a circular shape on a lightly floured surface. The shape will need to be larger than your dish, as it needs to form the sides of the pie also. Carefully lower this into the dish. Roll out the lid and set aside.

7 Mix the chicken, fennel mixture, mustard (if using), parsley and béchamel together. Take care when adding the béchamel – add a little at a time to get an idea of how much you'll need. Season the mixture with salt and pepper then fill the pie and top with the lid. You want the lid to overlap the sides of the pie dish. Crimp it down to make sure it's sealed. Cut a cross in the top with a knife and brush with the beaten egg.

8 Bake for 20–30 minutes at 200°C until golden brown.

Chicken and stuffing ball open pie

Dead easy, this one, and similar in construction to the meatball pie on page 83, only using chicken and stuffing. This recipe is great for when you've some leftover chicken from a roast. You can make this with entirely leftover ingredients, or from scratch. The recipe below calls for leftover chicken, but if you've not got any you could use a pack of skinless, boneless chicken thighs and chicken breasts and cook them (but by the time you've bought that you might as well have bought a whole chicken).

INGREDIENTS

- 350g cooked chicken meat
- 100ml of béchamel sauce (see page 52)
- Handful of frozen peas
- 1 tablespoon of chopped parsley
- 1 onion chopped
- 2 cloves of garlic crushed
- 30g butter
- 100ml milk
- 1 tablespoon of plain flour
- 1 packet of stuffing mix
- 1 packet of all-butter shortcrust pastry (or make your own, see page 32)
- Handful of strong cheese

METHOD

1 First make the stuffing balls. Rehydrate the stuffing as per the packet's instructions, and when cool enough to handle roll into little balls smaller than a ping pong ball and set aside.

2 Melt the butter in a pan and add the onion, cook for 5 minutes until soft then add the garlic. Add the flour and cook out until it thickens, then gently add the milk to make a roux (yes, the onion and garlic will be in there but that's OK).

3 Add the chicken meat, parsley and peas and combine. Cook for a further 5 minutes and set aside. You want enough of the béchamel to coat the meat but not so much that it's runny. If you find you've too much sauce (or not enough meat) you can always lift out the filling with a slotted spoon – this will allow any excess sauce to drain away.

4 Preheat your oven to 180°C.

5 Roll out your pastry, cut into a large circle and dust with flour. Transfer to a baking tray. (It's VERY important you do this before adding your filling). If the pastry cracks you're in trouble, so cut off any oddly shaped bits and have them by you in case you need to patch up any holes.

6 Start building up the filling in the middle, leaving a gap of around 5cm between it and the edge of the pastry. Finally, top with the stuffing balls. Gather the edges together and fold towards the middle. Add the cheese.

7 Quickly brush the outside of the pie with a beaten egg and place in a hot oven.

8 It's done after about 25–30 minutes or when the pastry is golden brown.

Chicken in a frying pan pie

The easiest pie in the world, this, as you make everything in one pan. Needless to say, it has to be a pan that you can put in a hot oven. I also use ready-made pastry as that saves time, mess and fuss too.

INGREDIENTS

For the filling
- ½ tablespoon of vegetable oil
- 1 small onion chopped
- 1 clove of garlic chopped
- Large handful of any leftover cooked chicken bits (thigh, breast or leg)
- ½ teaspoon of dried tarragon
- 100ml of chicken stock
- Tablespoon of crème fraîche
- Handful of frozen peas
- Leftover boiled/ roast potato

For the pastry
- 1 packet of pre-made, pre-rolled pastry (shortcrust or puff)
- 1 egg

I made this pie in a small 7in (18cm) frying pan, though I've done it in larger; if you're going to use a normal-sized frying pan double the amount of filling, and I'd probably use a pie bird in the centre. You can also use the tiny frying pans used for frying individual eggs, the result being more of a 'starter'-sized pie. You can also bulk out with leftover spuds.

METHOD

1 Place your pan on the hob and gently fry the onion in the oil until soft. Add the garlic halfway through (you don't want it to burn).
2 Add the chicken, tarragon, stock and crème fraîche and simmer for about 15 minutes until well combined. Add the potato.
3 Add the frozen peas and cook for another 5 minutes so they're cooked but still bright green.
4 Turn off the heat and leave to cool.
5 When cool, preheat your oven to 180°C. Take the pastry out of the packet and cut off two strips 1cm wide. Fashion these around the edge of your pan (this is to provide a bit more support to the pastry). Brush them with egg wash and unfurl your pastry over the pan. Crimp gently and trim

off the excess. Brush with the rest of the egg wash and place in the preheated oven for 15–20 minutes until the pastry is cooked and golden.
6 Allow to cool a little before eating straight out of the pan.

Massive Christmas pie

Historically these pies were, indeed, absolutely massive, and contained prodigious amounts of meat and game. Hannah Glasse gives this recipe in *The Art of Cookery, Made Plain and Easy* dating from 1747:

INGREDIENTS

For the filling

- Around 500g leftover turkey meat shredded
- 500g mixed game birds (pheasant breasts, pigeon breasts are available from good butchers during the winter months, duck is also readily available in supermarkets)
- 1 teaspoon each of the following spices, ground: mace, cinnamon, allspice berries, grated nutmeg, cloves (actually I don't like cloves, so I tend to leave them out)
- 300g of sausage meat
- 200ml of turkey stock made with the wings and carcass

For the pastry

- It's hot-water crust, fellas, and lots of it.
- 320ml boiling water
- 600g plain flour
- 600g strong flour
- 450g lard
- 1 tablespoon of salt
- 1 tablespoon of sugar

'First make a good standing crust, let the wall and bottom be very thick; bone a turkey, a goose, a fowl, a partridge, and a pigeon, season them all very well, take half an ounce of mace, half an ounce of nutmegs, a quarter of an ounce of cloves, and half an ounce of black-pepper, all beat fine together, two large spoonfuls of salt, and then mix them together. Open the fowls all down the back, and bone them; first the pigeon, then the partridge; cover them; then the fowl, then the goose, and then the turkey, which must be large; season them all well first, and lay them in the crust, so as it will look only like a whole turkey; then have a hare ready cased, and wiped with a clean cloth. Cut it to pieces, that is, joint it; season it, and lay it as close as you can on one side; on the other side woodcocks, moor game, and what sort of wild fowl you can get. Season them well, and lay them close; put at least four pounds of butter into the pie, then lay on your lid, which must be a very thick one, and let it be well baked. It must have a very hot oven, and will take at least four hours. This crust will take a bushel of flour.'

Now, that requires so many animals you'll probably get a visit from the RSPB – there's over eight different species in that. It isn't so much a pie as a pastry tomb for winter birds. Then there's the pastry – a bushel of flour is around 36kg. What must it have been like to not only afford one, but to present it to your friends, neighbours and household? How did they even cut it? They must have used a sword.

Anyway, let's make a more sensible version, as some of the flavourings are excellent. First off, it's time to talk turkey. We forget that turkey, too, is a game bird. Buying a good rare-breed naturally raised turkey is critical. It'll have the flavour, the

texture and the fat covering. Also, you don't have to bone out a whole one (that would take ages). Instead think of this as a deluxe version of a turkey pie.

You want to break out your biggest deep-sided, spring-loaded cake tin for this. I'm serious, this is the *big* one.

METHOD

1. Strip the meat from the turkey and make the stock from the carcass.
2. When the stock is ready, pass through a sieve to remove the bones and vegetables and pour about 200ml into a clean pan. Put the rest in the freezer for something else.
3. Poach the game meat in this stock for about 15 minutes until tender and cooked (this will help keep them moist).
4. Remove and leave to cool. Keep the stock.
5. Make your pastry (see page 38) and, working quickly, roll out and line your cake tin, saving enough to make the lid. Make sure it's well into the corners.
6. Then, in a bowl, mix the sausage meat with the cooked turkey and game meat and the spices. If it looks a little dry, add a spoon or two of the stock.
7. Fill the case with the filling and brush the edge with water.
8. Roll out your lid and place it on top. Cut a small hole for the steam to escape and bake in a moderate oven (160°C) for an hour. Check the filling is cooked with a meat thermometer and leave to cool completely before cutting into big wedges.

Venison pot pie

Ah, venison, the noblest of quarry. You don't have to be lord of the manor to enjoy this tasty, healthy, wild meat these days. It's available in most supermarkets and good butchers during the winter months. Indeed, this pie is the sort of thing to come home to after being out and about on a chilly winter's day; it'll warm your cockles no end. I've made it a pot pie here, with a puff pastry top, but you can use shortcrust and make it a double-cruster if you prefer. You can also cobble it.

INGREDIENTS

- 1kg diced venison
- 40g plain flour seasoned
- 2 carrots chopped
- 2 onions chopped
- 2 sticks of celery chopped
- 50ml of vegetable oil
- 50g butter
- 1 tablespoon of tomato purée
- 500ml beef or chicken stock
- Glass of port
- 8 juniper berries crushed
- Teaspoon of thyme leaves
- Zest of one orange
- 400g puff pastry
- 1 egg beaten

METHOD

1 First make the filling. Coat the meat in the seasoned flour, melt the butter and oil in a casserole and brown the meat in small batches, then set aside.

2 Add a bit more butter and oil to the pan if needed and then add the vegetables and cook. Add the tomato purée and get a good caramelisation going on.

3 Put the venison back in, add the port, stock, thyme, juniper and the orange zest and place in a 140°C oven for 3 hours minimum. When the meat is tender and the sauce has thickened, leave to cool then place in the fridge.

4 Transfer the filling to a pie dish. Preheat oven to 220°C.

5 Unroll the puff pastry and cut off a strip. Place this round the lip of your pie dish. Brush this ledge with the beaten egg and place your lid piece on top. Brush with the remaining egg and place in the oven for around 30 minutes or until the puff pastry has risen.

Rabbit pot pie

While it's never going to be as popular as chicken, rabbit is making a bit of a comeback. And this is a good thing. Part of the trouble with rabbit is that when it's on your chopping board it still looks like a dead, skinned animal, whereas a prepared chook sits the other way up and has had its head and legs lopped off.

INGREDIENTS

For the filling
- 1 tablespoon of vegetable oil
- 20g butter
- 2 rabbits (jointed up into pieces)
- 3/4 chunks of chorizo or other spicy sausage
- 2 medium onions chopped
- 1 carrot chopped
- 1 stick of celery chopped
- 1 teaspoon of thyme leaves
- 150ml of dry cider (or dry white wine)
- 500ml of chicken stock
- Salt and pepper

For the pastry
- Approx 300g of pastry
- 1 beaten egg

Some butchers have now caught on to shoppers' apparent squeamishness and offer rabbits ready jointed into legs and loin, all safely wrapped in plastic. Also, rabbits don't roast very well: they're far better braised in liquid until soft and tender. Which makes them perfect for pies. If you've not tried rabbit before, do so, you can now get it in some supermarkets, or any good butcher should be able to get it for you. Wild rabbit will have a stronger flavour than farmed, and need longer cooking time.

This recipe is based on a dish Tim Adams cooked for me at the River Cottage Cafe after I attended my father's funeral.

This recipe serves four in a small to medium-sized pie tin.

METHOD

1 Add the oil to a casserole and get it hot before browning the rabbit pieces all over. Remove and turn the heat down. Add the onions, carrot and celery, as well as the chorizo, and cook until soft. The chorizo will start to leech some of its lovely smoky oil.

2 Return the rabbit to the pot and add the stock, the cider and the thyme. Season well. Put the lid on slightly ajar and simmer on a low heat for 1½ hours until the rabbit is tender.

3 While the rabbit is cooking, make the pastry.

4 Remove the rabbit and the chorizo from the pan with a slotted spoon, and set aside to cool. Crank up the heat to reduce the sauce until a bit thicker. You can add a touch of crème fraîche at this point.

5 Shred the meat from the rabbit bones and put in a large bowl with the chorizo chunks. Add as much of the reduced sauce as needed to moisten the meat and allow to cool completely.

To assemble the pie

I'd probably serve this as a single-crust pot pie, topped with shortcrust (see page 32) or perhaps flaky (see page 36). But the filling would work equally well as double-crust. The filling should give you enough for a smallish to medium-sized dish or tin. You'll need approximately 200g for a single-crust pie in a medium dish.

6 Place the cooled filling in the dish, ensuring it comes up to the top. Brush the rim of the dish with the beaten egg and position your pastry on top. Crimp the edge and brush with the beaten egg. Make a little slit in the top of the pastry to let the steam out.

7 Bake in a hot oven (200°C) for 20–30 minutes until the pastry is golden brown.

8 Serve with more carrots – it's what the rabbit would have wanted – and mashed potatoes.

Partridge and pear pot pie

Ah-har! A pie worthy of Alan Partridge himself. The pears bring their customary sweetness while the birds offer some gamey notes. There are two types of partridge in the UK, the small native grey-legged and the larger, more common red-legged, which has a milder flavour. You could use pheasant if you prefer.

INGREDIENTS

For the filling

- 2 teaspoons of vegetable oil
- 10g butter
- 4 partridge breasts
- 2 onions chopped
- Pinch of thyme leaves
- 2/3 firm pears cored and chopped (Comice or Anjou would be good)
- 1 tablespoon of brandy (or Calvados or, even better, pear brandy)
- 1 tablespoon of double cream
- 200ml of dark chicken stock
- Salt and pepper
- 600g puff pastry

This recipe will make two to four pies.

METHOD

1. In a frying pan, heat the oil and the butter until bubbling, then add the partridge breasts. Don't move them, let them cook for 2 minutes each side, then add the brandy.
2. Tip the pan gently to one side and ignite the brandy, or light with a match. When the flames go out, remove the partridge.
3. Turn down the heat and add the onion and pear pieces and a glug more oil if it needs it, and cook until softened. Add the stock, thyme and the double cream. Season well and simmer until the sauce has reduced in consistency.
4. Cut up the cooled, rested partridge breast and return to the sauce to warm through. Taste, and add a drop more booze if you think it needs it. Turn out the heat and let cool.
5. Preheat your oven to 200°C.
6. When cold, make or buy enough puff pastry (see page 34) to cover four small pie dishes, about 150g per dish or 600g in total.
7. Fill your dishes with the cooled filling, and brush the rim of the dish with egg wash. Position the pastry on top and brush with the remaining egg wash.
8. Place in a preheated 200°C oven and cook for about 15–20 minutes until the pastry is puffed up and golden.

CHAPTER 6

FISH PIES

Fish, being more delicate than meat, needs judicious handling when you're putting it in pies. However, it's no slouch when it comes to flavour. The key thing is not to overcook it. Fish needs very little time to cook through. Of course, this means that you can rustle up something very quickly, rather than have to take hours making a slow-cooking stew. Don't ignore seafood such as mussels and prawns either – these not only back up the taste of the sea, they also offer a different texture to complement fish.

It goes without saying that although age equals flavour when it comes to meats like beef, it'll equal food poisoning when it comes to fish. You want the freshest fish possible.

Finally, please try to buy sustainably-caught fish. The issue of by-catch being thrown away because of quotas is terrible. Imagine if for every one cow we ate, nine were killed and left rotting in the field. There'd be outrage, yet this is what's happening at sea. Check the Marine Stewardship Council's website for the latest information.

Fish pie

Arrrgh! You can see the problem: should this fish pie recipe go in the fish chapter, or the potato-topped pies chapter that comes next? After all, a traditional fish pie is topped with spuds. In the end I decided to put it here, with the caveat that you can top it with pastry if you prefer, as well as potato.

INGREDIENTS
For the filling
- 700g assorted fish (cod, haddock, salmon, coley)
- 170g defrosted cooked seafood mix (muscles, prawns, squid)
- 1 bag of spinach
- 1 carrot
- 1 large handful of peas
- 1 medium onion chopped
- 1 leek trimmed and cut into rings
- 500ml full-fat milk
- 50g flour
- 100g butter

For the topping
- 1kg of floury potatoes (such as Maris Piper)
- Couple of knobs of butter
- Splash of milk or cream

Fish pie is another of those cheap, rustic dishes that are now neither cheap, nor particularly rustic. It is, however, proper tasty, as well as a family favourite. Another bonus is that you can use pretty much any combination of fish you can get your hands on (I'd avoid pike, carp and goldfish, however). Cheaper fish like coley can be used to bulk out the more expensive fish like cod and haddock. Get undyed smoked haddock, rather than the cheaper bright yellow one. Salmon too will add a dash of pink, as will prawns, but don't overdo it. I'd also avoid really oily fish like mackerel.

Veg-wise, I think you've got to have spinach, peas and carrots cut into small batons. Herb-wise, parsley is a must, as is fresh dill if you can get it. Don't bother with bay leaves or studding onions with cloves. Many recipes call for mushrooms, but I think they make the sauce grey, and their earthy taste doesn't really complement fish that well. Also, eggs are sometimes added, though I'm not sure they add much when weighed against the effort of boiling, cooling and shelling them. But add a few if you want to. Finally, a glug of white wine or, even better, vermouth takes things up a notch too.

This recipe will make enough for an A4-ish-sized large dish, which should serve six.

METHOD

1. Peel the potatoes and cut into large, even-sized chunks. Put in a pan of cold water and cook until they're tender, about 20 minutes. Peel the carrots and chop into small baton shapes.

2. When the potatoes are cooked remove them with a slotted spoon or drain but keep the water. Now cook your carrots in the potato water for 10 minutes. (You don't have to do this, you can just do them in another pan, but it saves time and energy.)

3. Drain the carrots, rinse and set aside.

4. Mash the now cooled potatoes (see page 166 for more tips on how to make mashed potatoes). Add the butter and the milk and beat. You want a fairly stiff mash, so go easy on the milk.

5. The final use for the saucepan is to wilt the spinach. Throw the spinach into the wet pan and put on a low heat to wilt down. Keep it moving – it should take about 5 minutes.

6. When it's all wilted, squash against the side of the pan with a spoon to get out any remaining moisture and set aside with the carrots.

7. Take a short break.

8. Put the chopped onion and leek in a frying pan with a little oil and cook until translucent. Remove and wipe out the pan. Put the fish pieces in the frying pan and pour the milk over them, bring to a simmer for about 8–10 minutes and quickly remove the fish to a plate to cool. Flake. Pour the milk into a bowl or jug and reserve.

9. Wipe out the pan, add 50g of butter and melt. Add the flour a dessertspoon at a time, and whisk around until incorporated. Now pour back in some of your reserved fishy milk to make a white sauce. Once made add the finely chopped parsley and dill if using.

To assemble the pie

10. Butter the sides of your ovenproof dish. Place the flakes of fish and cooked prawns in. Add the onion, the carrots, the peas and the wilted spinach.

11. Pour the white sauce over it, making sure everything is well coated.

12. Gently place the mashed potato in small amounts on top of the fish mixture. Don't press down too hard just yet. Smooth the mash together with a palette knife or the back of a spoon until the fish mix is entirely covered.

13. Run the tines of a fork along the mash to give you the telltale ridges. A handful of grated cheese can be added if you like.

14. All of this can be done in advance, or at this stage you can freeze it if you like. When you want to eat your fish pie, pop it in a hot oven (180°C) for 20 minutes until the mash on top is golden brown and the filling heated though.

15. You could serve with more peas, or maybe some watercress, but it's quite happy on its own.

Smoked fish pie with Cheddar mash topping

This recipe for mini fish pies is from chef Nathan Outlaw, whose restaurant has been named Best Fish Restaurant, so it's fair to say he knows a thing or two about fish. This is a great recipe for a wintry dinner party.

INGREDIENTS

For the filling
- 350g cod fillet skinned
- 350g smoked haddock undyed fillet
- 1 small onion
- 1 bay leaf
- 450ml milk

For the cheesy mash topping
- 1kg King Edward potatoes
- Salt
- 50g butter
- 200g Cheddar grated
- 200ml milk
- Pepper

For the white sauce
- 25g butter
- 25g plain flour
- 4 teaspoons of fresh parsley roughly chopped
- Salt and pepper

METHOD

1 Begin this fish pie recipe by placing the cod and haddock in a wide pan. Peel and quarter the onion and add along with the bay leaf to the fish. Pour the milk over.

2 Bring the milk up to the boil, reduce the heat and simmer for about 6 minutes. Remove the fish from the milk and place it on a plate.

3 Flake the fish into chunky pieces and divide into 8 individual ramekins. Sieve the milk into a jug and set aside to use in the white sauce.

4 Peel the potatoes and cut into 3cm chunks and place in a saucepan. Cover with water and add a pinch of salt. Bring the potatoes to the boil and simmer for about 20 minutes on a low heat.

5 When the potatoes are soft, drain, place them in a bowl and mash until smooth. Add the 50g of butter and 100g of the grated cheese as you mash.

6 Place the cold milk into a saucepan and bring to a simmer. Add this to the potatoes and beat. Season with salt and pepper. Once done, set the potato topping aside.

7 To make the white sauce, melt the butter in a pan, stir in the flour and cook for 1 minute over a moderate heat. Gradually add all the set-aside fish-poaching milk, whisking continuously.

8 Simmer for 1–2 minutes, stirring, until you have a smooth, slightly thick sauce. Remove the sauce from the heat, season with salt and pepper and add the chopped parsley.

9 Pour the sauce over the fish in the ramekins. Arrange the mashed potato over the top of the sauce and sprinkle on the remaining grated cheese.

10 Place in the oven at 180°C/Gas mark 4 and cook for about 30 minutes until bubbling and golden brown on top. Serve straight away.

Coulibiac

This dish was something of a '70s classic, and was a popular main course for dinner parties (one can imagine Alison Steadman serving it in Mike Leigh's *Abigail's Party*). Its origins are Russian, where it's made with salmon or sturgeon. There are a few stages to this recipe, but allow plenty of time and do it in stages and you'll be fine.

INGREDIENTS

- 75g butter
- 1 medium onion finely chopped
- 100g button mushrooms finely sliced
- 2 tablespoons of chopped dill
- 1 tablespoon of chopped parsley
- 100g cooked basmati rice
- 250ml of fish stock
- 1 teaspoon of ground coriander
- ½ teaspoon of cumin
- 1 lemon
- 3 boiled eggs, cooled, shelled and sliced
- 600g whole salmon fillet (you want a large piece, minimum 10cm long)
- 2 packs of ready-made rolled puff pastry

METHOD

1 Firstly, hard boil your eggs (about 8 minutes from a cold-water start; I use a little gadget that I pop in with the eggs that tells me when they're ready – never fails). Place in cold water when cooked and, while cooling, finely chop your onion and mushrooms.

2 Shell the eggs, slice and set aside.

3 Heat 20g of butter in a saucepan and sweat the onions until soft but not coloured. Add the mushrooms and cook until soft. Remove from the pan and set aside.

4 Heat another 10g of butter in the same saucepan, and fry the coriander and cumin, then add the fish stock, the rice and a squeeze of lemon and simmer on a low heat with a lid on the pan until the rice is cooked. Once cooked, drain any excess liquid and leave to cool. When cooled, mix in the onion and mushroom mixture.

5 Preheat the oven to 180°C. Brush a non-stick baking tray with a little oil and place in the oven. When hot, remove and place the salmon fillet on it. Put it back in the hot oven for 8 minutes. You don't want to cook it entirely, just get it going. Remove, and also leave to cool. (If you've a really big frying pan, you could do this stage in that.)

(All the stages so far can be done a few hours in advance.)

To assemble the pie

6 Beat an egg and have it ready.

7 Unfurl the pastry on to a floured surface and cut to about 5cm bigger than your salmon fillet. Transfer to a baking tray.

8 Place some of the cooked rice mixture in the centre and smooth out to about 0.5cm high and 5cm away from the pastry edge.

9 Gently place your salmon fillet on top.

10 Slice the eggs and place them on top of the salmon, then gently place the rest of the rice on.

11 Clear the 5cm border of any stray grains of rice and brush with beaten egg. Place the second slightly larger piece of puff pastry on top of the pie and cut to fit snug with the bottom piece. Make sure the filling is nice and snug to the pastry. Crimp the edge with the tines of a fork. You can adorn the top of the pie with letters, shapes or use a knife to gently mark a design in the surface of the pastry.

12 The whole thing can now be put back in the fridge for a few more hours, or cooked straight away.

13 To cook, brush with the remaining egg wash and bake in a preheated 200°C oven for 20 minutes, before turning down to 180°C for another 15–20 minutes until golden brown.

14 Leave to cool before serving. To serve, cut into slices, or just sent to table on a big board and let everyone dive in.

Mackerel rolls

Dead easy, these, as you can make them entirely from ready-made ingredients. They're kind of like a fishy sausage roll. They're inspired in part by a drawing in Dorothy Hartley's excellent book *Food in England*, though hers had the whole head sticking out. These rolls are great for picnics too.

This recipe serves four.

INGREDIENTS

- 1 packet of four hot smoked mackerel fillets (the vacuumed-packed ones, not ones in tins)
- 1 spring onion or small bunch of chives
- Tablespoon of crème fraîche
- A little lemon zest
- Teaspoon of horseradish
- 1 packet of pre-made shortcrust pastry
- 1 egg to glaze
- Sesame seeds (optional)

METHOD

1 Finely chop the spring onion. Remove the skin from the cooked mackerel fillets and flake into small pieces. Add the zest, the horseradish and the crème fraîche and combine in a bowl. You're after a stiffish mix.

2 Preheat oven to 200°C.

3 Roll out the chilled pastry on a floured surface. Cut four pieces, each about the size of a medium-sized envelope (about 10cm by 7cm).

Place the mackerel mix along one edge and roll up. Trim off the ends and squash down with a fork to seal in the filling. Brush with egg wash, and scatter the top with sesame seeds (or black poppy seeds would be nice).

4 Bake in the oven for 15 minutes until the pastry is golden. Serve with pickled onions, cornichons, gherkins or even stewed gooseberries! You need something sharp to contrast the oily fish and biscuity pastry.

Crab pot pies

Crab is a lovely meat, and these days you can get really good crab meat in tins without the faff of dressing out yourself. The white claw meat is more expensive than the brown, but like chicken, I think the dark meat is where the flavour is. So use a can of light and dark if possible

This recipe serves two.

INGREDIENTS

- Knob of butter
- 4 shallots finely diced
- 2 tins of shredded crab meat
- 1 very finely chopped spring onion
- 1 finely chopped red chilli
- 1 small bunch of finely chopped coriander
- 2 tablespoons of double cream
- 1 egg beaten
- 200g ready-made puff pastry

METHOD

1. Melt the butter in a pan and sweat the shallots until tender but not coloured. Turn off the heat and add the chilli and spring onion. Then add the crab meat, coriander and cream and combine until you have a whitish filling flecked with green and red. Spoon into two ramekins.
2. Cut two strips of pastry to form collars around the lip of your ramekins. Brush the lip with egg wash, place the collars on, and then brush these with egg wash too, before placing on your lids. Trim off any excess pastry and make a small vent in the top.
3. Place in a preheated oven (200°C) for 10–15 minutes until the pastry is cooked.
4. Remove and leave to cool.

Dressed crab pot pies

Another idea you might want to try is making the pot pie in the crab's shell rather than a ramekin:

a. Buy a ready-dressed crab presented in its shell. Spoon out the meat and mix with coriander, chilli, spring onion and a little fish stock, double cream or even white sauce, and spoon it all back in.

b. Take a piece of puff pastry and cut about 3cm bigger than the shell. Brush the shell with egg wash and place the pastry on top.

c. Brush the pastry, cut a small vent in the top, and place in a preheated 200°C oven for 10–15 minutes until the pastry has puffed up and turned golden. Leave to cool and serve.

Salmon and dill pie

The classic combination of salmon and dill are joined by watercress in this light summery pie. It's similar in construction to the mince lamb filo pie on page 72. You can serve it hot or cold, perhaps with some sweet nutty new potatoes and a salad. Who says pies can't be classy?

This recipe serves four.

INGREDIENTS

- 1 tablespoon of vegetable oil
- 1 medium onion diced
- 1 clove of garlic crushed
- 4 large salmon fillets chopped into large chunks
- 1 bunch of dill finely chopped
- 1 bunch of watercress, stalks removed
- 100ml crème fraîche
- Juice of half a lemon
- Salt and pepper
- 1 packet of filo pastry

METHOD

1. Heat the oil in a pan and gently cook the onion until soft but not coloured.
2. Add the garlic and cook for a further 5 minutes, then add the salmon pieces. Don't move them around too much. You just want to start them off cooking.
3. Add the watercress and wilt a little, and finally the crème fraîche, lemon juice and the dill. Season well and leave to cool.

To assemble the pie

4. Melt the butter in a microwave or saucepan and have it standing by along with a pastry brush.

You have to work quickly with filo as you don't want it to dry out.

5. Brush one sheet of filo with the melted butter and place in a shallow ovenproof pie dish. You want the edges to hang over the lip of the dish.
6. Brush another sheet and place the other way, and repeat a third time.
7. Add the salmon filling and smooth down.
8. Fold the overhanging edges of the filo into the centre, and brush again with the melted butter. If it needs it, add one more well-buttered sheet of filo on top.
9. Press down gently, then bake in a preheated oven (180°C) for 20 minutes until golden brown.

Prawn cocktail pies

Inspired by the retro classic that is a prawn cocktail, I've used similar flavours in this simple pie filling. It can be served hot or cold. Serve with a big dollop of irony, and a green salad.

This recipe makes around ten pies.

INGREDIENTS
- 20g butter
- 1 clove of garlic finely chopped
- 2 large banana shallots finely chopped
- 400g peeled cooked jumbo prawns
- 300ml crème fraîche
- 1 pinch of paprika
- A couple of shakes of Tabasco sauce
- 1 teaspoon of tomato ketchup
- Half a lemon squeezed
- 1 tablespoon each chopped dill and flat-leaf parsley
- 3 sheets of ready-made puff pastry
- 1 egg beaten

METHOD
1. Melt the butter in a saucepan and gently cook the shallots until soft but not coloured.
2. Add the garlic and cook for a further 5 minutes. Leave to cool a little then add the cooked prawns, the crème fraîche, the Tabasco, the ketchup, the lemon juice and the herbs. Allow to cool completely.
3. Remove and unfurl your pastry from the packet and, using a large ramekin or mug as a guide, cut out 20 discs of pastry. (An even better idea would be to use a scallop shell).
4. Spoon some of the filling into the centre of each dish, brush the edge with egg wash and fix on a lid. Crimp the edges down. When all 10 are made, chill for 10 minutes.
5. Preheat oven to 200°C.
6. Brush pies with the remainder of the egg wash and place on a baking tray in a hot oven for 12–15 minutes until the pastry is cooked and the pies are golden.

Mini tuna pies

Dead cheap, and pretty easy to make, these pies are sort of like a vol-au-vent with a lid. It's best to make these in a Yorkshire pudding tin. Perfect for picnics too.

INGREDIENTS

- 2 tins of chunky tuna drained
- 1 small spring onion finely sliced
- 1 red chilli finely diced
- 40g butter
- 35g flour
- 200ml milk
- 1 beaten egg
- Salt and pepper
- 250g of puff pastry

METHOD

1 First make a béchamel sauce (page 52). Melt the butter in a pan over a low heat and add the flour. Cook for 5 minutes until the flour is well combined, then add the milk, stirring constantly until the sauce thickens.

2 Finely chop the spring onion and the chilli and put in a bowl with the tuna. Spoon the béchamel sauce over and combine. Season and leave to cool.

3 Unfurl your puff pastry, and, using a ramekin, pastry cutter or large mug as a guide, cut out 12 discs.

4 Preheat oven to 180°C.

5 Place six in a non-stick Yorkshire pudding tin and spoon some of the filling into each. Run around the rim with egg wash (you may need a paint brush rather than a pastry brush for this!) and place the lid on. Crimp the edge with a fork and place in the oven for 10 minutes until the pastry is cooked and golden brown. Leave to cool before serving.

CHAPTER 7
POTATO-TOPPED PIES & COBBLERS

Potato-topped pies are the easiest type of 'pie' to make. They keep well, freeze well, and you don't need to make any accompaniments bar boiling some frozen peas as a side. The two titans among spud-topped pies are the classic shepherd's and cottage, and on the following pages you'll find recipes and the history of each.

Both of those feature mashed potato, but there are also pies topped with thin slices of potato, such as the Lancashire hot pot. You can use a ceramic dish for these pies, and they'll help keep it warm when taken to the table.

Whenever you're making a potato-topped pie, always let both topping and filling cool down a bit before putting one on the other. If your filling's still hot and very runny your potato could be in danger of sinking in. Another tip is to apply the potato in small amounts first, building it up slowly – if you dollop the whole lot in it'll just sink down and push the filling up. Finally, if you do really want a pastry fix you can 'cobble' any of these fillings rather than use potato.

Shepherd's pie

Although we now think of shepherd's pie as being made only with lamb, while cottage pie (page 119) is made with beef, this wasn't always the case. Early recipes describe how any leftover cold meat can be used. Other recipes go on to describe the potato topping on a cottage pie as ridged (perhaps like the thatch of a cottage), while on a shepherd's pie it's smooth.

INGREDIENTS

For the filling

- ½ tablespoon of sunflower oil
- 1 large onion, diced
- 2/3 medium carrots, diced into cubes
- 1 stick of celery diced
- 500g lamb mince (or any leftover roast lamb trimmed of fat and diced into pieces)
- Large dash of Worcestershire sauce
- 500ml stock (chicken or beef)
- 1 teaspoon of tomato purée
- ½ teaspoon of dried thyme
- ½ teaspoon of cornflour to thicken the gravy
- Salt and pepper

For the topping

- 1kg potatoes cut into chunks
- 90g butter
- Splash of milk
- Handful of grated cheese (optional)

The first printed recipe for a shepherd's pie that we'd recognise appears in *Practice of Cookery and Pastry* by an Edinburgh cookery teacher called Mrs I. Williamson, published in 1854. Both cottage and shepherd's pie seem to have evolved out of using up leftovers from the Sunday roast, and this is still a very fine idea, though these days we no longer have huge Victorian families to feed. Finally, if you make your pie with Quorn or soya mince it's apparently known as a 'shepherdess' pie'.

This recipe serves four and fills a medium to large pie dish.

METHOD

1 Peel the carrots and onion and chop into a fine dice along with the celery. Peel and chunk the potatoes. Bring a pan of water to the boil and add the potatoes.

2 Heat the oil in a frying pan on a high heat and fry the lamb mince in small batches and remove. Turn the heat down and fry the onion, carrot, and celery in the pan until softened.

3 Return the mince and add the stock, dried thyme, Worcestershire sauce and tomato purée. Mix the cornflour with a little water and add to thicken up the gravy a little.

4 Simmer on a low heat for 30 minutes (sometimes I cook the filling in the oven; if you'd rather do this, pop it in for an hour at 130°C).

5 When the sauce has reduced and it all looks lovely, it's done. Place an inch depth of filling in your dish and leave to cool.

6 Meanwhile keep an eye on the spuds – follow the recipe for mashed potato (page 166). It's very important to let them steam dry after draining off the water, otherwise you'll have too wet a mash.

To assemble the pie

7 Remember, let your mashed potatoes and filling cool a little before putting the former on the latter. Start by applying little blobs of potato using a tablespoon, dotting them around on top of your filling. If you put the whole lot in, it'll sink like a bowling ball.

8 Gradually add more blobs until they start to join together. Then, with the back of a spoon or a palette knife, smooth the potato together.

9 You can now run a fork down the length of the pie to make grooves, though some Victorians would no doubt object. A handful of cheese on top makes things extra special.

10 Place in a preheated oven at 180°C for 20 minutes until the potato is golden brown and the filling hot.

Cottage pie

Cottage pie gets its first mention in 1791, so predates the young shepherd's by a considerable number of years. Interestingly some recipes for cottage pie (and ideas for shepherd's) call for a layer of potato *underneath* the filling as well as on top.

INGREDIENTS

For the filling

- ½ tablespoon of sunflower oil
- 1 large onion, diced
- 2/3 medium carrots, diced into cubes
- 1 stick of celery diced
- 500g beef mince (or you could use shin of beef chopped finely with a knife)
- Large dash of Worcestershire sauce
- 200ml beef stock
- 300ml ale or beer
- 1 teaspoon of tomato purée
- ½ teaspoon of dried thyme
- ½ teaspoon of cornflour to thicken the gravy
- Salt and pepper

For the topping

- 1kg potatoes cut into chunks
- 90g butter
- Splash of milk
- Teaspoon of horseradish (optional)

Today recipes for both pies are similar in ingredients bar the change of meat. However, I think a good cottage should include things that improve beef's robustness; consequently I add beer to the filling, and a spoon of grated horseradish to the mash. I'm not a big fan of adding tinned tomatoes to cottage pie filling – I think this turns it into something more like a bolognese sauce. Instead use good quality meat, stock and beer to give maximum flavour.

This recipe serves four and fills a medium to large pie dish.

METHOD

1 Peel the carrots and onion and chop into a fine dice along with the celery. Peel and cut up the potatoes. Bring a pan of water to the boil and add the potatoes.

2 Heat the oil in a frying pan on a high heat and fry the beef mince in small batches and remove. Turn the heat down and fry the onion, carrots and celery in the pan until softened.

3 Return the mince and add the stock, beer, dried thyme and tomato purée. Mix the cornflour with a little water and add to thicken up the gravy a little.

4 Simmer on a low heat for 30 minutes (sometimes I cook the filling in the oven; if you'd rather do this, pop it in for an hour at 130°C).

5 When the sauce has reduced and it all looks lovely, it's done. Place an inch depth of filling in your dish and leave to cool.

6 Meanwhile keep an eye on the spuds – follow the recipe for mashed potato (page 166). It's very important to let them steam dry after draining off the water, otherwise you'll have too wet a mash.

To assemble the pie

7 Remember, let your mashed potatoes and filling cool a little before putting the former on the latter. Start by applying little blobs of potato using a tablespoon, dotting them around on top of your filling. If you put the whole lot in, it'll sink like a bowling ball.

8 Gradually add more blobs until they start to join together. Then, with the back of a spoon or a palette knife, smooth the potato together.

9 Adding a layer of seasoned breadcrumbs over the mash turns a cottage pie into a Cumberland pie, apparently.

10 Place in a preheated oven at 180°C for 20 minutes until the potato is golden brown and the filling hot.

Lancashire hot pot and Cumbrian tattie pot pie

Lancashire hot pot (much beloved by *Coronation Street*'s Betty Williams) is a classic dish of the North-West. Head a little further north and it morphs into Cumberland tattie pot.

INGREDIENTS

- 30g butter
- 800g diced lamb (or mutton if you can get it)
- 1 large carrot cut into chunks
- 3 large onions finely sliced
- 2 teaspoons of plain flour
- 900g potatoes, peeled and finely sliced (about as thick as a one-pound coin)
- 800ml light chicken stock

Lancastrian chef Nigel Haworth knows a thing or two about making hot pot; his version was selected for the *Great British Menu*'s main course in series 7. Nigel recommends using a mix of shoulder, neck and shin from the animal. He also favours mutton over lamb, though sadly mutton isn't as easy to come by as it once was. You can also make hot pot with a combination of diced lamb and a few lamb chops.

There's a purity to a good hot pot that lets the flavour of the lamb and potatoes shine through – some recipes you'll see call for wine, tomato purée and all sorts of other ingredients that certainly weren't in the pantry of your average 19th century Lancastrian miner or mill worker.

A hot pot is traditionally made in an earthenware dish with a lid, though you can also use a metal casserole dish.

METHOD

1 Heat half the butter in a casserole until melted and brown the lamb meat. Remove and set aside. Add the sliced onions, cook until softened and remove. Add the flour and cook a little in any remaining butter and fat (this will eventually thicken the sauce later, along with the starch from the potatoes).

2 Add back to the pan a layer of lamb, then onion, then lamb, then onion. Season well with salt and pepper. Then pour the stock over it.

3 Arrange the potatoes in a layer up towards the top of the dish.

4 Melt the remaining butter in the microwave and, using your pastry brush, brush the top potato layer with butter. Cover with the lid and place in a low oven, about 150°C for about 2 hours until the potatoes are cooked.

5 Remove the lid and put under the grill to brown the top layer of potatoes. Let it cool a moment before serving. Serve with pickled cabbage.

Individual gnocchi-topped fish pies

This recipe came about when I made a fish pie (page 104) and had some of the cooked filling mix left over but not enough of the mash (I think I'd added a few extras to the filling, or maybe not had enough potatoes).

INGREDIENTS
- Around 300g of fish pie mix (or any filling you have that you want to top with potato)
- 1 pack of gnocchi
- Handful of hard cheese (pecorino would be good)
- 2 teaspoons of butter

Now, I could have rustled up some pastry and made a pastry-topped version – nothing wrong with that. But I didn't fancy getting the flour and butter out. What I did get out, though, was a pack of gnocchi from the freezer.

This recipe serves two, though of course you could up the quantities and make it serve four if you wanted.

METHOD

1 Divide your leftover filling between two ramekins and set aside.

2 Cook the gnocchi as per the packet instructions. When they're almost done (a matter of moments if not frozen) – basically, when they float to the top – quickly drain and add the butter to the hot empty pan.

3 Return the gnocchi to the pan and swirl round to melt the butter. This process will stop your gnocchi from sticking together.

4 Working as quick as you can, take each gnocchi and place 'end up' in the filling. Start at the edge of the ramekin and work round into the centre.

5 When they're all in place grate the cheese over them. (Note you can freeze them at this stage – defrost them before cooking, though.)

6 Place in a hot oven around 180°C for 10–15 minutes until the cheese has melted and the peaks of the gnocchi have crisped up a little.

Coquilles St Jacques

These were popular in the 1970s, but I think it's about time they made a bit of a comeback. They're not that hard to make – you just need to get your hands on some good scallops as well as their shells (though you could use an ovenproof saucer if you can't get the latter). Some recipes call for a breadcrumb topping, so feel free to adjust if you like. You'll also need a piping bag – you can buy disposable ones from the cake section of any supermarket.

This recipe will make four.

INGREDIENTS

For the filling
- 8 dressed scallops and their shells (white muscle and roe removed)
- 200g button mushrooms
- 100ml of white wine
- 100ml fish stock
- Squeeze of lemon juice
- 1 tablespoon of chopped parsley
- 1 tablespoon of plain flour
- 3 tablespoons of double cream
- 50g grated Gruyère cheese

For the mashed potato
- 500g potatoes (floury ones such as Maris Piper)
- 100g butter
- ½ teaspoon of nutmeg
- 3 egg yolks
- Salt and white pepper

METHOD

1 Have four of the shells cleaned and ready – you want the curved side, not the flat one. Then make the mashed potato (see page 166). After you've mashed it and it's cooled slightly, add the nutmeg, salt, pepper and the egg yolks and beat together until no lumps remain and it's light and fluffy.

2 Put the largest nozzle in the piping bag and fill with the mashed potato. Pipe a border around the edge of each of the shells and leave to cool (you might want to practise on a saucer first).

3 Preheat the oven to 200°C.

4 Place the scallops, the stock and the wine in a frying pan and gently poach until the scallops are just turning white. Remove the scallops with a slotted spoon and set aside.

5 Remove the liquid, add a knob of butter to the pan, add the mushrooms and the lemon juice and two tablespoons of the reserved cooking liquid. You don't want to fry the mushrooms, just poach them so they keep their whiteness. When they're cooked, remove and set aside.

6 Add the remaining butter to your pan and add the flour to make a roux (page 52). Instead of adding milk add some of the reserved cooking liquor. When ready, finish with the double cream, half the cheese, salt and pepper, and the parsley.

7 Cut the scallops into bite-sized pieces, add to the sauce along with the mushrooms and combine.

8 Using a tablespoon, spoon the mixture into the centre of each of your shells surrounded by the mashed potato and sprinkle the rest of the cheese over them. Place in the hot oven for around 15 minutes until the potato is golden, the sauce bubbling and the cheese melted.

Beef and Guinness cobbler

If the thought of making a double crust pastry pie scares the bejeezus out of you, then you could try this recipe first. Cobbler dough is just blobs of dough placed on top of savoury or fruit fillings. Made with self-raising flour, they puff up like little scones or biscuits, and provide that pastry hit to contrast with the filling underneath. You need a good firm stew to hold the dough; if your filling is too liquid they'll sink. Also, don't fanny around with fancy biscuit cutters and whatnot – a cobbler should look rustic.

INGREDIENTS

For the filling

- Beef dripping (or oil if you're being boring)
- 1.2kg of stewing beef or shin
- 3 medium onions sliced
- 3 carrots peeled and cut into large chunks
- 2 sticks of celery diced
- Teaspoon of thyme leaves
- 500ml Guinness or other stout
- 500ml of beef stock
- 2 tablespoons of seasoned flour
- Salt and pepper

For the cobbler

- 225g plain flour
- 4 teaspoons of baking powder
- 100g butter
- Handful of grated strong Cheddar
- Teaspoon of finely chopped rosemary
- Pinch of salt and pepper
- 2–4 tablespoons of milk

Very much a pie for a winter's day, this. You can make the filling in advance, then just rustle up the cobbler dough when needed. You could use the filling recipe for beef and ale pie (page 63) and just cobble it.

METHOD

1 Add the dripping to a casserole and melt. Add the onions, carrots and celery to this and cook until soft and the edges start to caramelise. Remove and set aside, and add more dripping to the pan.

2 Toss the beef in the seasoned flour and fry in small batches until coloured on all sides. Remove.

3 Add a splash of the stout to get any nice bits off the bottom of the pan, then return the meat, herbs and vegetables to the pan. Add the rest of the beer and stock and season well.

4 Bring up to a boil then place in a medium oven (140°C) for about 2½–3 hours until the beef is tender and the sauce reduced. (If your sauce is too runny stir in a teaspoon of cornflour mixed with cold water to thicken). Leave to cool.

5 Make your cobbler dough (see page 42) and add the herbs and cheese. Shape the wet dough into golf ball-sized balls, then squash flat to hockey puck-sized discs or just spoon blobs of it over the stew. Place on the surface of your cobbler, with perhaps a third of their height below the surface (this means their bottoms will be nice and soggy). Brush the tops with some milk. They'll expand as they cook, and the joy of the cobbler is seeing gaps between each scone.

6 Bake in a hot oven (180°C) for about 30 minutes until they've risen and turned a golden brown.

CHAPTER 8

VEGGIE PIES

Until the Victorian age, those that chose not to eat meat were known as Pythagoreans, after the famous (and non-meat-eating) mathematician. And much as I love eating a good meat pie, it doesn't hurt once in a while to go meat-free.

Most commercial vegetable pies I've found are rather dull and disappointing. The key I've found with meat-free cooking is to ramp up the additional supporting flavours, and vary the size and texture of the other ingredients. That way you're getting interesting tastes as well as a different feel in the mouth. Come to know the power of the mighty mushroom, and explore the world of strongly flavoured vegetarian cheeses (the British Cheese Board lists over a hundred vegetarian cheeses that don't use animal rennet in their production process); both of these will complement your vegetables. Finally, I think if you're going to do a meat-free pie you shouldn't bother with protein-based meat substitutes – they'll only remind you of what you've left out.

Spanakopita

If you're veggie and you've been on holiday to Greece, you've probably ordered this classic Greek spinach pie dish. It uses filo pastry (though you could make it with puff). The spinach mix is really versatile, and can be used as the filling in a toastie, or in stuffed peppers. Check your teeth after eating, as spinach is a right one for getting between them.

INGREDIENTS

- 900g spinach (two large bags)
- 10 small shallots peeled and finely chopped
- 1 tablespoon of finely chopped parsley
- 1 tablespoon of finely chopped spring onion
- 100ml olive oil
- 4 eggs beaten
- 250g crumbled feta cheese
- Zest of a lemon
- 1 pinch of nutmeg
- 12 sheets of ready-made filo pastry

Filo dries out in moments, so keep it between two clean, damp tea towels until you need it.

METHOD

1 Heat a little of the oil in a large pan (with a lid) and gently soften the shallot; remove and set aside. Add the washed spinach and cook down for five minutes. Drain in a colander and, using the back of a spoon, squeeze out any remaining moisture.

2 Return the spinach to the pan and warm on a low heat for a few moments to thoroughly dry out. Add the cooked shallot, crumbled feta, nutmeg, lemon zest and the beaten eggs.

3 Brush a shallow rectangular pie or flan dish with the olive oil and lay on the first sheet of filo. Brush with more oil and lay another sheet the other way. Repeat six times so your bottom pastry layer is six sheets thick.

4 Spread the spinach and cheese mixture over the pastry base.

5 Add the remaining six sheets of filo, always brushing each of them with oil.

6 Bake in a hot oven (180°C) for 25–30 minutes until the pastry is golden brown.

7 Leave to cool for a few moments before cutting into large squares and serving.

Magical mushroom pie

'Make room for the mushroom!' went the jingle for an advert in the 1980s extolling the virtues of the fabulous fungus. And it's true, the mighty 'shroom can pack a lot of punch, particularly the porcini.

INGREDIENTS
For the filling
- 2 teaspoons of vegetable oil
- 800g mixed fresh mushrooms
- 3 large (or banana) shallots finely chopped
- 2 cloves of garlic crushed
- Handful of dried porcini mushrooms
- 1 teaspoon of fresh thyme leaves
- Salt and pepper
- Dash of mushroom ketchup (optional)

For the sauce
- 25g butter
- 20g flour
- 150ml milk
- Reserved porcini liquor
- 20ml white wine (optional)

The key with mushrooms is to use a variety: a few dried porcini, some whole button mushrooms, long pieces of portobello – you get the idea. You want different sizes, shapes, textures and intensity of flavour. You'll also need a lot of them to make a decent amount of filling, as they shrink when cooked. They also exude a lot of liquid.

Onion, thyme, and strong (blue) cheese are other flavours that complement mushrooms, along with cream and fortified wine like sherry.

This recipe makes enough filling for one large pie or four individual pies.

METHOD
1 At least an hour before you start cooking, rehydrate the porcini in 50ml of warm water (you can even do this overnight). When they've plumped up, remove with a slotted spoon and reserve. Strain the water through a tea strainer or a sieve lined with kitchen paper to catch any bits, and reserve this too.
2 Put the oil in a large frying pan and gently soften the chopped shallots. When they're nearly done, add the mushrooms and move around the pan. They'll look like they're not doing much at first, but keep the heat gentle and they'll begin to break down. Add the garlic and thyme at this point. When the mushrooms look cooked, turn off the heat.
3 In a saucepan make a béchamel sauce (page 52). Before you add the milk, add the reserved porcini liquor, the wine if using, then top up with milk to get a smooth sauce. Add as much of this as you think necessary to ensure the mushrooms are all coated. Leave to cool.

To make the pastry
4 The type of pastry is your choice. A rough puff (page 35) lid on a shortcrust bottom (page 32) would work well here. Or make into individual pies.
5 Cooking times will slightly vary accordingly. For a large shortcrust-topped version it'll need about 30 minutes in a 180°C oven. Puff pastry (see page 34) will need a hotter oven and a shorter cooking time.

Lord Woolton pie

Woolton pie was created by Savoy maître-chef François Latry (1919–42 – a small pencil drawing of him hangs in the National Portrait Gallery) and named after the Liverpool businessman and head of the Ministry of Food during World War Two, Lord Woolton. It was his job to keep the nation fed, and as well as this he's also the man responsible for the national loaf and Government cheese. And so what little was left of our rural artisan foods were finally seen off during WW2.

INGREDIENTS

For the filling
- 300g potatoes
- 2 carrots
- 2 parsnips
- Half a swede
- Half a head of cauliflower
- Teaspoon of oatmeal

For the pastry
- 200g plain wholemeal flour
- 100g butter (but during WW2 this would have been any fat you could get)
- 3 tablespoons of cold water
- Pinch of salt

With meat being rationed and severely limited, Woolton pie was intended to inspire housewives to get creative in the kitchen. As vegetarians like to repeatedly point out, with animal fats, cheese and meat all rationed, the population was healthier during and after the War – but were they happy? (Incidentally, the other dish that became popular during the War, and has remained so, was carrot cake, though now we add sugar and fat back in, whereas originally the carrots provided most of the 'sweetness'.)

Anyway, here's the original recipe as it appeared in *The Times* on 26 April 1941: 'Take 1lb (453g) each of diced potatoes, cauliflower, swedes and carrots; Three or Four spring onions; One teaspoonful of vegetable extract and One teaspoonful of oatmeal. Cook all together for ten minutes with just enough water to cover. Stir occasionally to prevent the mixture from sticking. Allow to cool; put into a pie dish, sprinkle with chopped parsley and cover with a crust of potatoes or wholemeal pastry. Bake in a moderate oven until the pastry is nicely brown and serve hot with brown gravy.'

Now, I don't know about you, but I don't think that the diced potatoes will be cooked through in just ten minutes in 'just enough water to cover'. Also it seems odd to use spring onions, rather than ordinary brown ones. Still, there was a war on.

So here's my version of Woolton pie, which remains fairly faithful to the original. The aim is to produce a cheap, healthy pie, right? Well the thing about vegetables is they're often dead cheap in season. If you pick up mange tout from Africa or courgettes from Israel in November, they're not going to be cheap. Stick to British root veg, however (particularly in the cooler months), and it'll cost you pence. Also, vegetables that are steamed rather than boiled retain more of their nutritional value; steaming potatoes, however, takes ages.

METHOD

1. Make the pastry by combining flour and salt then adding the fat and working together with your fingers. Add the water and combine. Chill before using.

2. Peel and dice the potatoes, parsnips and swede and put into a pan with cold water. On top, place a steamer and add the cauliflower florets, peeled carrots cut into small batons and a handful of peas from the freezer. Boil the root veg while steaming the other vegetables on top. When the root vegetables are cooked, drain them, saving some of the cooking water.

3. Add the potato water to oatmeal and simmer for 10 minutes until swollen and cooked, and approximating a sauce. (To be honest béchamel would be better, if you can get your hands on some more black market butter, flour and milk from a GI; perhaps wouldn't be as healthy, though.)

4. Add the filling to a pie dish, and cover with the wholemeal pastry. Bake in a preheated hot oven (180°C) for 30 minutes until the pastry is brown. Let it stand a moment before eating. A blob of brown sauce would improve morale on the home front.

© Jassy Davis

Bubble and squeak pie

A good chef should always, always cook too much Sunday roast. That way you get lots of leftover cabbage, peas, carrots, mashed swede and roast potatoes, as well as meat and gravy. All but the last two can be put to use in bubble and squeak pie (sadly, when it's encased in pastry you won't be able to hear the whistling and squeaking as it's cooked which gives the dish its name). This is unashamedly a leftovers pie – don't set out to make this from scratch, that would be madness.

INGREDIENTS

For the filling

- Around 600g of assorted leftovers (roast potatoes, carrots, peas, cabbage, parsnips, mashed anything – whatever you've got kicking about; if you've not got enough, bulk it out with some frozen peas, or a tin of cannellini beans)
- 100g of vegetarian Cheddar grated
- Salt and pepper
- Handful of chopped parsley
- 30–50ml vegetable stock, veggie gravy or water, just to moisten the filling
- 1 beaten egg

For the pastry

- 200g ready-made puff pastry, or use shortcrust (page 32) if you prefer; or do a shortcrust bottom with a puff pastry top

This recipe will make one medium-sized pie.

METHOD

1 Because everything's already cooked you don't really have to do much to get this filling together. Just chop up your leftovers into bite-sized pieces and mix in a bowl with the cheese, parsley, plenty of seasoning and a little water or vegetable stock to moisten.

2 Cut about a third of the pastry away and save for the lid. Roll out the remainder and line your tin. Trim off the edge and spoon in the filling.

3 Roll out the lid. Moisten the edge of the pie with egg wash and place the lid on. Brush with egg wash and bake in a hot oven (180°C) for around 30 minutes until the pastry is golden brown.

Cauliflower and broccoli cheese pie

This follows a similar construction technique to the meatball pie (page 83) and the stuffing ball pie (page 95), only it contains big chunky florets of two of my favourite brassicas, cauliflower and broccoli. It's essentially a cauliflower cheese, but with broccoli added to provide a bit of contrasting colour.

INGREDIENTS

- ½ head of cauliflower cut into florets
- ½ head of broccoli cut into florets
- 50g butter
- 45g flour
- 300ml milk
- Teaspoon of English mustard
- Handful of grated strong vegetarian cheese
- 1 pack of ready-made and rolled shortcrust pastry

METHOD

1 For best results steam the vegetables until al dente rather than boil them – this will help them stay firmer and be less soggy. The cauliflower will take a few minutes longer than the broccoli, so put that in the steamer above a pan of boiling water first. (If you've not got a steamer fit a sieve over the pan and use a lid on top.)

2 Make the roux (page 52) and add the cheese, stirring until melted. Leave to cool.

3 Roll out your pastry, cut into a large circle and dust well with flour. Transfer to a baking tray. (It's VERY important you do this before adding your filling.) If the pastry cracks you're in trouble, so keep the trimmings to patch up any holes.

4 Start building up the cauliflower and broccoli in the middle, leaving a gap of around 5cm between it and the edge of the pastry. Gather the edges together and fold towards the middle. Pour the sauce into the large hole in the top and scatter more grated cheese over.

5 Quickly brush the outside of the pie with a beaten egg and place in a hot oven (180°C).

6 It's done after about 25–30 minutes or when the pastry is golden brown and the cheese sauce all bubbling.

Mixed bean cobbler

If you don't eat meat you're probably well acquainted with using pulses in your cooking. And while packets of dried ones may be cheaper, for speed and value you can't beat a few tins of beans. Like mushrooms, the key is to use a variety of shapes, sizes, colours and textures. You also need something to stand against their creamy, earthy, soft taste, so in this recipe I've gone down the spicy and tomato route. You could, however, play around with a white wine-based sauce, thinly sliced fennel and herbs like tarragon and parsley.

INGREDIENTS

For the filling
- Glug of vegetable oil
- 3 cans of beans (pick a combination of butter beans, kidney beans, borlotti beans, even chickpeas)
- 2 medium onions chopped
- 2 cloves of garlic chopped
- 1 can of chopped plum tomatoes
- 100ml of vegetable stock
- 1 teaspoon of hot smoked paprika
- 2 chillies chopped
- Dash of smoked Tabasco sauce
- 1 teaspoon of treacle (trust me, this is the secret ingredient)
- 1 teaspoon of white wine or cider vinegar

For the cobbler dough
- 225g plain flour
- 4 teaspoons of baking powder
- 100g butter
- Handful of grated strong vegetarian Cheddar
- Pinch of salt and pepper
- 2–4 tablespoons of milk
- 10ml of milk

METHOD

1 Add the oil to a casserole pan and gently fry the onion until soft.
2 Add the garlic, the beans drained of their water, the can of tomatoes and all the other ingredients.
3 Leave on a low heat to simmer for 40 minutes, stirring occasionally until the sauce has reduced and all the ingredients are well combined. Leave to cool (this stage can be done a day in advance). Depending on the size of your casserole, you might want to transfer to a deep baking dish before adding the cobbler dough.
4 Make your cobbler dough (see page 42) and add the cheese. Shape the wet dough into golf ball-sized balls, then squash flat to a hockey puck-sized disc, or just spoon blobs of it over the stew. Place on the surface of your cobbler, with perhaps a third of their height below the surface (this means their bottoms will be nice and soggy). Brush the tops with some milk. They'll expand as they cook, and the joy of the cobbler is seeing gaps between each scone.
5 Bake in a hot oven (180°C) for about 30 minutes until they've risen and turned a golden brown.

Cheese and onion pie

The classic combination of cheese and onion is too good to leave to a packet of crisps. Put some effort into your cheese choice on this – you want to use a hard, aged cheese with plenty of flavour. Many recipes call for Lancashire (part of the crumbly cheese family that includes Wensleydale and Cheshire), and that's what I've used here. But if you're one of those people who thinks it tastes like soap, use something else, like a good Cheddar.

INGREDIENTS

- 1 tablespoon of vegetable oil
- Knob of butter
- 3 medium onions finely sliced
- 2 eggs
- 250g grated Lancashire cheese
- Salt and pepper
- 350g shortcrust pastry (page 32)

This is essentially a flan with a lid, rather than a deep-dish style pie. Consequently it's best made in a round, shallow 8in (20cm) flan or cake tin.

Recipe serves four to six, the pie being best served cut into wedges.

METHOD

1 Add the butter and oil to a large frying pan and gently cook the onions without colouring them until soft and tender. Keep them moving so they don't stick. They'll take a while – don't rush them.
2 When cooked, remove and spread out on a plate or clean chopping board to cool down.
3 In a bowl mix the cooled onion, the grated cheese, salt and pepper, and one of the eggs well beaten. (Resist the temptation to add some diced bacon, but if you do want to add any extra flavourings, now's the time.)
4 Preheat oven to 180°C.
5 Remove a third of your pastry and set aside. Roll out the rest and line the tin with it. Add the onion mix and smooth out. Brush the edge of your base with the second egg beaten. Roll out your lid and place on top. Crimp and trim the edge and brush the top with the remainder of the beaten egg. Snip a small hole in the top to let out any steam.
6 Place in a hot oven for 30–40 minutes until golden brown. Allow to cool a little before serving.

Tomato Tatin pie

Ah, the Tatin sisters – little did they know, when they created their eponymous dish, that others would replace the traditional apples with everything from bananas to tomatoes. And why not? It's a great idea, and a simple way to combine seasonal ingredients with pastry. If you've not made a Tatin before, don't worry – they're dead easy, but you do need a frying pan that can go in the oven. I make my Tatins in a small 8in (20cm) frying pan. (For more Tatin recipes, see pages 141 and 159.) This recipe serves two.

INGREDIENTS

- 1 tablespoon of olive oil
- 1 tablespoon of butter
- Pinch of sugar
- Pinch of salt
- 1 red onion finely sliced
- 3 very ripe vine-ripened tomatoes
- 5 cherry or baby plum tomatoes
- 1 clove of garlic crushed or finely chopped
- Salt and pepper
- A few thyme leaves
- Basil leaves
- 1 packet of puff pastry

METHOD

1 Add the oil to the pan and then the onions, salt and sugar and cook gently until they're soft but not coloured. After five minutes add the garlic. When cooked, remove and set aside. Slice the large tomatoes equatorially, the small ones any way you like.

2 Add the butter to the pan, melt it, place the tomatoes cut side down and cook gently – you don't want them to burn, just get a little colour on them. Use the small ones to fill in the gaps between the larger ones. After a few minutes scatter the cooked onions over the tomatoes in the pan.

3 Preheat the oven to 200°C.

4 Roll out the pastry and, using a small plate just a bit bigger than your pan, cut a round disc. Place this on top of the tomatoes and tuck the edges down inside the pan. Cook for 25–30 minutes until the pastry has risen up, then leave to cool for five minutes.

5 Place a large plate over the pan and, using oven gloves or tea towels, flip it upside down and give it a little shake. The tomatoes are now on top of the pastry.

6 Garnish with the basil leaves and eat while still warm.

CHAPTER 9
THINGS THAT ARE ALMOST PIES

Where pie stops and other things begin is a bit of a grey area. It's not just about being sealed in pastry, otherwise cottage pie wouldn't be called a pie, while Cornish pasties and salmon en croûte would. What follows are things that are distant branches of the pie family tree – dishes like pasties and salmon en croûte that evolved for much the same reasons as pies did, using pastry to keep their fillings contained and safe. I suppose in its very loosest sense a pie is a combination of two things, a 'filling' and some contrasting outer carbs, either pastry or potato-based. Mind you, by those rules the wafer cone under some ice cream might be considered a pie! (It's not though, clearly.)

Defining what exactly *is* a pie therefore gets tricky. So perhaps it's best to wander off into the kitchen and do some cooking.

The Cornish pasty

After a nine-year battle, the Cornish pasty finally won PGI (Protected Geographical Indication) status, meaning they have to be made in a certain way, to a certain set of ingredients and, most importantly, they have to be made in Cornwall. They must be a D shape, and crimped at the side, not the top. Inside the meat must be chunky, made from uncooked minced or roughly cut chunks of beef (not less than 12.5%), swede, potato, onion, and a light peppery seasoning.

The recipe given here, which will make four pasties, comes from the body charged with protecting the production of Cornish pasties, the Cornish Pasty Association, so you can rest assured it's a 'proper job'.

INGREDIENTS

For the filling
- 450g good quality beef skirt, cut into cubes
- 450g potato diced
- 250g swede diced
- 200g onion sliced
- Salt and pepper to taste (2:1 ratio)
- Beaten egg or milk to glaze

For shortcrust pastry*
- 500g strong bread flour (it's important to use a stronger flour than normal, as you need the extra strength in the gluten to produce strong, pliable pastry)
- 120g lard or white shortening
- 125g Cornish butter
- 1 teaspoon salt
- 175ml cold water

All images © the Cornish Pasty Association

* Rough puff can also be used.

METHOD

1 Rub the two types of fat lightly into flour until it resembles breadcrumbs.
2 Add water, bring the mixture together and knead until the pastry becomes elastic. This will take longer than normal pastry but gives it the strength that's needed to hold the filling and retain a good shape. This can also be done in a food mixer.
3 Cover with cling film and leave to rest for 3 hours in the fridge. This is a very important stage as it's almost impossible to roll and shape the pastry when fresh.
4 Roll out the pastry and cut into circles of approximately 20cm diameter. A side plate is an ideal size to use as a guide.

5 Layer the vegetables and meat on top of the pastry, adding plenty of seasoning.

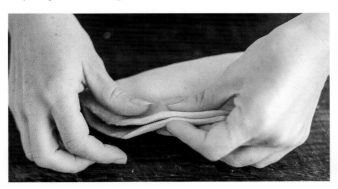

6 Bring the pastry around and crimp the edges together (see the guide to crimping below).
7 Glaze with beaten egg or an egg and milk mixture.
8 Bake at 165°C (fan oven) for about 40–45 minutes until golden.

Top tips

• Beef skirt is the cut traditionally used for Cornish pasties. This is the underside of the belly of the animal. It has no fat or gristle, cooks in the same amount of time as the raw vegetables and its juice produces wonderful gravy.
• Use a firm waxy potato such as Maris Peer or Wilja. A floury potato will disintegrate on cooking.

HOW TO CRIMP

Crimping is one of the secrets to a true Cornish pasty. A good hand-crimp is usually a sign of a good handmade pasty. To crimp a Cornish pasty:

1 Lightly brush the edge of the pastry with water.
2 Fold the other half of the pastry over the filling and squeeze the entire half.

3 Push down on the edge of the pasty, and using your index finger and thumb twist the edge of the pastry over to form a crimp.

4 Repeat this process along the entire edge of the pasty.
5 When you've crimped along the edge, tuck the end corners underneath.

'Three in a bed' pie

Bit of a wheeze this one. Indeed, I'm not sure it's even a proper pie. It's great fun, mind. It's sort of like a sausage roll, only with three sausage bits rather than one. You don't have to stop at three either. Feel free to add more 'in the bed'. It's a great one for a kids' party – in fact, why not get them to help make it?

INGREDIENTS
- 3 (or more) jumbo sausages
- 1 packet of ready-made puff pastry
- 1 beaten egg

You could cheat and use hot dog sausages, but they're disgusting and mainly made from mechanically recovered chicken slurry. Buy some good quality extra-large or jumbo-sized sausages. They need to be big, as ordinary-sized ones will look a bit lost.

METHOD
1 Grill, fry or bake the sausages as the packet describes and leave to cool.
2 Preheat oven to 190°C.
3 Roll out the pastry into a rectangle about half the size of a piece of A4 paper. Place the cold sausages snugly along the top with their 'heads' resting on the top of the pastry. Fold up the bottom half of the pastry to form their duvet, and crimp down slightly between each sausage. Brush with beaten egg.
4 Put on a baking tray in the hot oven and cook until the pastry is puffed up like an eiderdown and golden brown (about 15–20 minutes).
5 Serve on a big wooden chopping board with chips and peas and let the kids sing 'there were three in the bed and the little one said' as they tuck in.

Extras
You could get a bit more creative here if you like. Try scoring a diamond pattern on the 'duvet', or why not fry off some onions and put them under the sausages to form hair? Finally, you can buy edible eyes made from black and white sugar frosting if you want to give your sausages faces. Sound nuts I know, but believe me, the kids will love it.

Sausage rolls

Homemade sausage rolls still warm from the oven with a blob of English mustard and a glass of good beer are about as good a snack as a chap can hope for. Poorly made cheap commercial ones, on the other hand, are horrible. It's the way they coat the roof of your mouth with that claggy film, and the way they don't really taste of anything.

INGREDIENTS

- 6 or 8 good quality sausages
- 1 pack of ready-rolled puff pastry (or make flakey p36)
- One small onion finely grated (or you could blitz in a food processor; alternatively finely dice it and fry it gently in a little oil before adding to the sausage meat)
- Any herbs you fancy (finely chopped sage is nice; you could also add diced apricot, or nutmeg, onion marmalade, more salt and pepper, curry powder, grated cheese – anything really, except perhaps Space Dust (now *there's* an idea!).

You've got two choices when making sausage rolls: one, unleash your inner butcher and mince your own pork from scratch (see page 59); or two, cheat by buying really good bangers, squeezing out the meat and pimping it with a few flavoursome extras. As you can imagine, I generally favour the latter approach.

METHOD

1 Squeeze the meat from your sausages into a bowl and add any extras you're using. Add the onion and mix well. Tip out on to a board and roll back into three sausage shapes about 4cm thick.

2 Unroll your pastry and cut lengthways into three long strips about 8cm wide.

3 Preheat the oven to 200°C.

4 Place each sausage meat piece on a strip of pastry lengthways and roll the pastry over, sealing with beaten egg. Roll each cylinder on the bench to ensure a nice round sealed shape, then place with the edge facing down on a non-stick baking tray.

5 Brush with the remaining egg wash and pop into the hot oven for about 20 minutes until the pastry is golden brown. Serve with mustard, curry or chilli sauce and a few beers.

Cumberland sausage Tatin

Anything you can cook in a pan, you can 'Tatin' I reckon. And that goes for sausages as much as it does apples (page 159) and tomatoes (page 133). What you need for this is a big, round coil of Cumberland sausage, though a South African *boerewors* would work OK too. This is best made in a small frying pan that holds the sausage snugly in it.

This recipe will serve two.

INGREDIENTS
- Knob of butter and glug of oil
- 3 medium onions finely sliced
- 1 coiled sausage
- 1 packet of puff pastry

METHOD

1 Heat the oil and butter in a pan and gently cook the onions until soft. Remove and set aside. To make it easier to flip the sausage over during cooking, thread a wooden skewer though it and place in the pan with a drop of oil. Cook gently until the surface is caramelised and brown, then flip over and colour the other side. When this is done remove the skewer, scatter the cooked onions over the sausage and allow to cool.

2 Preheat the oven to 200°C.

3 Roll out your pastry and, using a plate slightly bigger than your pan, cut a round disc.

4 Place the pastry on top of the sausage and tuck down the edges inside the pan.

5 Place in a hot oven and cook for about 25 minutes until the pastry has risen and is golden brown.

6 Allow to cool slightly. Place a large plate over the pan and, using oven gloves or tea towels, flip it upside down and give it a little shake. Serve with gravy (page 168) and some mashed potatoes (page 166).

Beef Wellington

Whilst it's not a pie in the traditional sense, a beef Wellington is certainly a stunning dish and a great showpiece to put on the table. It's quite technical to make, and not cheap either, as it uses fillet steak; but pull this off and no one will ever doubt your kitchen credentials again.

INGREDIENTS
- 800g–1kg fillet of beef
- 4/5 ready-made pancakes
- 2 cloves of garlic finely chopped
- 2 shallots finely chopped
- 400g chestnut mushrooms finely chopped
- A few dried porcini mushrooms rehydrated
- 100g of smooth pâté
- Small bunch of parsley finely chopped
- 2 tablespoons of double cream
- 1–2 packets of ready-rolled all-butter puff pastry (have a spare, just in case)
- 1 beaten egg

You'll see all over the Internet that it's named after Arthur Wellesley, the first Duke of Wellington (1769–1852), but it isn't; nor is it anything to do with Wellington, New Zealand, or Wellington boots. Indeed, the recipe doesn't appear in any English cookbook until the 1970s, though the *Oxford English Dictionary* has a reference from a restaurant in New York in the 1930s. It is, in fact, just a classic *filet de bœuf en croûte*.

METHOD

1 First, sear the beef. A mini project in itself, this. Get a pan as hot as you can and add vegetable oil. When the oil starts to shimmer add the beef fillet and gently roll around to colour on all sides. You want the beef to be cooked on the outside, but still pink in the middle – this will vary depending on the thickness of your fillet. Also you can't really tell unless you cut it open. Generally I've found it takes longer than you think, and a medium Wellington is better than one that oozes blood everywhere. Alternatively you can roast the fillet in a 230°C oven for around 15 minutes. The reason for doing this is that when the completed Wellington goes into the oven, it's really only to cook the pastry. There's not really time to cook the fillet further.

2 Once you've done that, leave it to cool.

3 Next make the duxelles. This is basically a mushroom paste that provides extra flavour. You can either finely chop all the ingredients by hand, or blitz the whole lot up in a food processor. Once you've got your minced mushrooms and shallots, fry them in a little oil until soft, drain off any liquid, and add the cream and the parsley. Cook for a further 10 minutes until the pan is quite dry, then leave to cool. When cold, mix with the pâté.

To assemble

4 Lay a piece of foil on the work surface and place 3 or 4 pancakes overlapped in a row slightly longer than the length of the beef fillet. Spread the cooked mushroom mixture on them. Place the cooked, cooled fillet on top and fold the pancakes over to cover the fillet. Trim off any bits that cause you trouble. Use the foil to help you shape the pancake around the beef. Don't press too hard or your mushroom mixture will ooze out.

5 Unfurl the puff pastry and place the pancake-wrapped fillet in the centre. Fold the edges over and seal them with egg wash.

6 Place back on the foil and chill for 20 minutes while the oven gets hot. Preheat oven to 220°C and put your baking tray in the oven.

7 Place the Wellington with the sealed edges down, brush with the remaining egg wash, place on the hot baking tray and cook for 25 minutes until the pastry is cooked and golden brown.

8 Leave to cool slightly before serving. Cut into 1in (2.5cm) slices and, with any luck, your beef fillet will be pink and juicy in the middle.

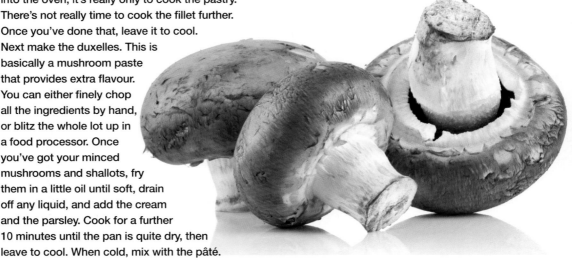

Pork Wellington

Similar to the beef Wellington above, only a bit smaller and much cheaper. Indeed, it's worth practising on pork before moving up to beef. Unlike the beef version, you want your pork cooked all the way through, rather than rare.

INGREDIENTS

- 350g pork fillet
- 2/3 ready-made pancakes
- 1 bag of spinach wilted
- 1 tablespoon of double cream
- Grate of nutmeg
- 2 cloves of garlic finely chopped
- 2 shallots finely chopped
- 200g chestnut mushrooms finely chopped
- A few dried porcini mushrooms rehydrated
- 50g of smooth pâté
- Small bunch of parsley finely chopped
- 2 tablespoons of double cream
- 1 packet ready-rolled all-butter puff pastry
- 1 beaten egg

You can play about with it too. Try adding crumbled black pudding into the mushroom mixture rather than pâté; some dried fruits like apricot would also work. Here I've added a layer of wilted spinach leaves to give a flash of green in the centre.

METHOD

1 First, seal the pork fillet in a hot pan as you would for a beef Wellington, and leave to cool.

2 Wilt the spinach in a large pan and squeeze out any water in a sieve, mix with the cream and a grate or three of nutmeg, and set aside.

3 When the fillet is cold, slit down the centre top to bottom, open out slightly with little cuts to make a sort of pocket, and stuff the wilted spinach mixture in the centre.

4 Make the mushroom mixture as you would for beef Wellington.

5 Lay 2 or 3 overlapping pancakes on a board and spread the cooled mushroom mixture on them. Place the fillet on top and roll the edges of the pancakes over to seal. Trim off any extra bits.

6 Unroll your puff pastry and check for cracks. Place the pancake-wrapped fillet in the centre and wrap the edges over, sealing with egg wash. Egg wash the top as well.

7 Turn over and place on a baking tray (you can chill it again at this stage if you like). Preheat oven to 220°C and place the Wellington in the hot oven for 20–25 minutes or until the pastry is golden brown.

Salmon en croûte

We've done beef and pork, so now it's fish's turn. Oddly we don't call this a salmon Wellington, but salmon en croûte.

INGREDIENTS

- 500g salmon fillet from the thick end of the fillet sliced into two, or two pieces from the thinner end that are the same size and shape
- 1 large shallot finely diced
- 3 handfuls of fresh spinach and watercress
- 1 tablespoon of crème fraîche
- 2 teaspoons of butter
- Juice of half a lemon
- Small bunch of parsley finely chopped
- Salt and pepper
- 1 packet of puff pastry (375g)
- 1 egg beaten

METHOD

1 Starting with the right piece of fish is important. Speak to your fishmonger or the person at the fish counter if you don't fancy doing it yourself. You're splitting the fish so the spinach and watercress mixture can be placed in the middle.

2 When you've got your fish prepared, make the spinach and watercress mixture. In a large frying pan add the spinach and watercress and wilt. When broken down transfer to a sieve and squeeze out any remaining water.

3 In the pan, gently fry the shallot in a little butter, and when soft transfer to a bowl. Add the wilted spinach and watercress, the crème fraîche, the lemon juice and the chopped parsley. Mix and season well.

4 Place one piece of the fish on a piece of cling film, and spread the spinach and watercress mixture over it. Place the other piece of fish on top, wrap tightly in cling film and chill while you get the pastry ready.

5 Preheat the oven to 220°C.

6 Make, roll out, or simply unroll your pastry. You're after two pieces about an inch bigger than your piece of salmon, with the top piece being slightly bigger. Place the bottom piece on a sheet of greaseproof paper. Take the fish out of the cling film and place it on the bottom piece. Brush the rim with egg wash and place the top piece on firmly, ensuring there are no pockets of air. Trim off any overhanging pastry and crimp the edge with a fork. Brush with the remainder of the beaten egg. Transfer to a baking tray.

7 Place the salmon en croûte in the hot oven and cook for 20–25 minutes or until the pastry is golden. Leave to cool a little before serving. Boiled new potatoes and a white wine sauce with more blitzed-up watercress in it are the best accompaniments.

Bedfordshire clanger

The Bedfordshire clanger is unique in that it's savoury at one end and sweet at the other. It's basically a two-course meal in a one-foot long pastry case. You can 'clang' any two ingredients together, and this recipe from Street Food expert Andy Bates sees tasty beef at one end and sweet juicy pears at the other.

INGREDIENTS

For the filling

- 2 tablespoons of vegetable oil
- 2 onions finely chopped
- 500g beef skirt chopped
- 1 tin of beef consommé
- 1 tablespoon of Worcestershire sauce
- 2–3 ripe pears peeled, cored and roughly chopped

For the pastry

- 300g–350g self-raising flour
- 1 teaspoon of salt
- 85g shredded beef suet
- 60g butter chilled and coarsely grated
- 1 free-range egg
- 150ml water

METHOD

1 Make the meaty bit of the filling: heat half the vegetable oil in a large, heavy-based frying pan and gently cook the onions for two to three minutes until soft and translucent. Remove from the pan and put to one side.

2 Heat the pan again over a high heat, add the rest of the vegetable oil, season and add the chopped meat. Cook over a high heat for three to four minutes, turning, until evenly browned. Remove the meat from the pan and mix with the onions.

3 Add the stock to the pan together with the Worcestershire sauce and boil until you have only two to three tablespoons left. Then add the meat and onions back to the pan and cook over a high heat until the sauce has reduced and is just coating the meat. Remove from the heat and leave to cool.

4 Preheat the oven to 200°C/Gas mark 6. Meanwhile, make the pastry: mix the flour, salt, suet and grated butter with your fingers into a fine breadcrumb-like consistency. Mix in about 150–160ml water and the beaten egg to form a smooth dough, and knead it for a minute. Roll the pastry on a floured table to about ½cm thick, cut into rectangles about 12–14cm long by 8cm wide and brush the edge of the long end with beaten egg. Retain any of the pastry cut-offs.

5 Next, spoon the meat filling into one half and the pear into the other, using a little piece of moulded spare pastry to separate them in the centre. Roll the pastry over into a large sausage roll shape, place on a lightly greased or non-stick baking tray and brush with the beaten egg. You can mark one end at this stage so that you don't get mixed up between sweet and savoury.

6 Bake for 45 minutes, or until the pastry is golden.

Snickers en croûte

Yes, you heard right. This is where things get mucky. You can wrap anything in pastry, even chocolate bars. Obviously they need to be ones with a fair bit of structural rigidity – an Aero, for instance, would disintegrate into bits. The key thing is making sure your pastry is tightly sealed around your bar, with no gaps or holes for anything to ooze out.

INGREDIENTS
- 6 chocolate bars
- 500g of ready-made puff pastry
- 1 beaten egg to seal and glaze

The second key thing is to bake it in a hot oven, to cook the pastry before the bar starts to melt and liquefy. If you're thinking of doing these for a dinner party, you're mad (though there's something rather amusing about asking 'Anyone for Toblerone en croûte?' They are, however, great for a kids' party, though if that's your intention you'd be better off using 'fun-sized' bars rather than normal-sized ones.

This recipe will serve six.

METHOD
1 Roll out your pastry into rectangles about 3cm bigger than each bar.
2 Place the chocolate bar upside down on the pastry, fold the two

longest edges over first so that they just overlap, and seal together with egg wash. Fold the two ends under and seal with egg wash. Turn over and place on a baking tray. Repeat for all six bars then place back in the fridge to chill.
3 Preheat the oven to 200°C. Egg wash the tops of the bars and bake in the oven for 20 minutes until pastry is puffed up and golden.

Kids will probably want ice cream with it.

CHAPTER 10

SWEET PIES

Now, if you've had pie for your main course, more pie for pud might be a bit too much. That's OK. Just keep these sweet pies in mind when you fancy a pie hit. Anyway, sweet pies can be smaller and lighter than big, communal meaty versions. What's more you can often have just a slice, perhaps with a cup of tea at four o'clockish. Mmmm.

You can also make single-crust sweet pies, but have a choice whether to do single-crust on top or single-crust underneath. Technically the latter makes it a tart or a flan, but historically many things that are actually tarts or flans are referred to as pies.

When making fruit pies it's always worth having a few tins of fruit in the cupboard as a back-up, just in case some of your fresh apples, plums or whatever are a little on the small side, or you loose one or two due to bruised bits. Frozen fruits are also handy, particularly cherries and blueberries. You can pick up frozen fruit mixtures that are perfect for pies quite cheaply, and augment them with fresh ingredients, or indeed with anything on the turn in the fruit bowl.

Apple pie

A man can devote a lifetime to endlessly striving for the perfect apple pie. After all, there are so many variables: the type of pastry, the type of apple, the ideal shape and structure, and finally the choice between ice cream and custard. Here's how I like to make mine...

INGREDIENTS

For the filling

- 4 big Bramley apples (about 1kg)
- 2 dessert apples
- 30g caster sugar
- Pinch of cinnamon (two if you like it)
- Pinch of nutmeg
- Tablespoon of apple juice (or cider, thinking about it!)
- Teaspoon of cornflour (optional depending on the ripeness of your apples – see method)

For the pastry

- 400g plain flour
- 100g butter
- 100g lard
- 30g caster sugar
- Pinch of salt
- A few tablespoons of cold water

The pastry has to be homely shortcrust – puff just doesn't work here. Also, I like to use lard in my sweet shortcrust. If the idea is strange to you, substitute an equal amount of butter. The apples, I feel, need to be a combination of mainly cookers (Bramleys) and a few dessert. The former mush down to almost a sauce, while the latter stay firm to provide a filling. And it most definitely has to be custard that you serve with it, or cream at a push. This is a double-crust pie.

Apple pie is best served warm, rather than piping hot from the oven, so allow plenty of time to make it. This recipe should make enough for a round 9in/22cm pie tin. As with most recipes, adjust your pastry and filling to fit your dish.

METHOD

1 Make the shortcrust pasty by putting the flour and sugar in a bowl and rubbing in the fat. Add a little water and combine to form a dough. Bring together and squash into a lozenge shape, wrap in cling film and chill.

Optional extras

There's an old saying that 'an apple without cheese is like a kiss without a squeeze'. If you'd like to introduce cheese to your apple pie you can either add 50g of grated Cheddar to the pastry, or a crumbly cheese like Wensleydale to the apple mix. Needless to say, I'd avoid serving with custard if you go down this route.

2 Peel and core the Bramleys and cut into chunks. Peel and core the dessert apples and slice as thinly as you can. Place the Bramleys in a saucepan with a drizzle of apple juice, cider or even water to stop them sticking, and put on a low heat. Add the sugar. Watch them, as Bramleys will turn to mush on a sixpence.

3 Now, how watery is your apple mix? If your apples are particularly ripe or if you prefer a firmer filling you might want to add a little cornflour to thicken and set your filling. When you're happy with it and the Bramleys have begun to mush down, add the slices of dessert apples and gently push down into the Bramley mush. Cook for another few minutes. Remember, it'll set a little when it cools, so put the lid on and leave to cool. You're after a balance of tartness from the Bramleys and sweetness from the dessert apples.

4 Get the oven up to 180°C. Beat one egg in a cup and have it standing by. Remove a third of the pastry and place back in the fridge. Roll out the remaining two-thirds to line your pie dish – don't cut the overhanging excess, just neaten it up so you can get it in the oven. With a pastry brush, paint the pastry with the beaten egg. This will help stop any apple juices from leaking into your pastry. Place the tin in the hot oven for a few moments (3–4 minutes) to set the egg. Then remove.

5 Place the filling into the pie, trim the excess pastry and roll out the remaining third of the pastry to make the lid. Use the rest of the beaten egg to seal the lid on to the pie. Brush the lid with the rest of the egg, and dust it with some more caster sugar. Cut a small hole in the top to let any steam out.

6 Place in the oven and cook for 45–50 minutes until golden brown. Remove and let cool for a good 20 minutes before you even think about cutting it.

7 Serve with custard (page 175), obviously.

Cherry pie

'Kent, sir – everybody knows Kent – apples, cherries, hops and women,' said Charles Dickens of that county. Sadly Kent doesn't produce anywhere near as much of the first three as it used to, though travelling through the county in midsummer you can often still see people selling cherries in lay-bys. Sussex and Hertfordshire are two other big cherry-producing counties in the South-East.

INGREDIENTS

For the pastry

- 400g plain flour
- 100g butter
- 100g lard
- Pinch of salt
- 30g caster sugar (and a sprinkle more for on top)
- A few tablespoons of cold water
- Beaten egg to glaze

For the filling

- 500g stoned cherries
- Teaspoon of booze (kirsch or brandy)
- 1 tablespoon of cornflour
- 20g caster sugar

Cherries have a short season – just two months, July and August. Consequently this is one of those pies that you should only make if you happen on a glut of them. You need at least a good-sized boxful, 500g at least. Look out for sour cherries such as Morello rather than dessert ones.

If you're going to have a go I'd also recommend a cherry stoner, which can be had for about a fiver online, as de-stoning a kilogram of cherries by hand with a knife will send you insane. Alternatively you could use tinned or frozen cherries. Just don't try it with the glacé variety.

I think a shallow pie dish similar to a plate works best for this, but use whatever dish you're comfortable with.

METHOD

1 Make the sweet shortcrust pastry by putting the flour and sugar in a bowl and rubbing in the fat. Add a little water and combine to form a dough. Bring together and squash into a lozenge shape, wrap in cling film and chill. Alternatively make it in a food processor, or use ready-made. Get your oven up to 180°C.

2 Mix the stoned cherries, cornflour and sugar together in a saucepan and heat gently. You don't want them to turn to mush, just soften them up a bit. The cornflour should help thicken the sauce. Once they're softened, set aside to cool.

3 Cut off a third of the pastry and reserve for the lid. Roll out the remainder and line your pie dish. Prick the bottom with a fork, line with baking parchment, tip on your baking beads and blind bake for 7–8 minutes. Remove and brush with beaten egg, return to the oven for a minute to set the egg. Trim off any excess or overhang.

4 Place your cool cherry filling into the pie dish and brush the lip with beaten egg. Roll out the lid and place on top, crimping it carefully to the base. Brush with the rest of the beaten egg and sprinkle some sugar over it.

Mucky mouth pie

The main ingredient in this pie is wimberries (also known as bilberries, whortleberries or winberries), which grow wild on the moorlands of the Pennines. Their season is very short, just a few months of early summer. Traditionally children would head out to the hills to pick the berries, and their habit of eating as many as they picked saw their faces splattered with the juices, hence the name of this pie. If you can't get bilberries you can use blueberries or damsons.

INGREDIENTS
- 350g sweet shortcrust pastry (see page 32)
- 1 Bramley apple peeled, cored and sliced
- 2 dessert apples peeled, cored and thinly sliced
- 400g winberries
- 100g caster sugar
- 1 egg beaten

This recipe serves six to eight. It's best made in a round, shallow pie tin with a removable bottom.

METHOD
1 Cut a large third off your pastry and set aside for the lid of the pie.
2 Roll the remainder out on a floured surface to fit your pie tin.
3 Preheat oven to 180°C.
4 Add greaseproof paper and baking beads and blind bake for 15 minutes. After 10 minutes remove the paper and beads, brush the base with egg and turn the oven off. The filling can be quite moist in this pie, so you want a firm bottom before adding it. Trim off any overhanging excess and leave to cool.
5 In a bowl mix the wimberries, slices of apple and sugar.
6 Add the filling to the pie case, making sure it's well packed in.
7 Turn the oven down a little to 170°C.
8 Roll out the remaining pastry to form a lid.
9 Brush the edge of the pie case with egg and place the lid on.
10 Wash the top with the beaten egg.
11 Bake in the oven for 25 minutes until the pastry is golden.
12 Leave to cool a little before serving with cream.

Mince pies

Mince pies are to be found everywhere at Christmas time, from budget versions to fancy filled ones, but you can't beat rubbing up your own batch for when the hordes descend. These are the pies to get your novelty cutters out for – you can play around with the tops. Also, I'd recommend adding a drop of brandy to the mincemeat. Kids hate mince pies anyway, so you don't have to worry about them. You could also add more fruit, and chocolate chips too (not traditional, but nice). You'll need a 12-cavity pie tray.

INGREDIENTS

- 500g shortcrust pastry (see page 32)
- 350g mincemeat
- Slug of brandy
- Caster sugar for dusting
- Milk

METHOD

1 Roll out the pastry and, using a 2in (5cm) cutter, cut 12 discs and place them in the tray. Gather the remaining pastry, roll out again and cut 12 lids with a slightly smaller cutter.

2 Place a dessertspoon of mincemeat in each bottom case. Brush a little milk around the rim of each pie and place a lid on.

3 Dust with the caster sugar and bake in a hot oven (180°C) for 15–20 minutes. Apply a little more caster sugar.

4 Best served warm with drinks, friends and relatives.

Cumberland rum nickies

The port of Whitehaven in Cumbria is responsible for introducing tropical flavours such as rum, molasses and spices to many Cumbrian dishes, and the rum nicky is no exception. You can either make this as a shallow double-crust pie and cut it into pieces, or as a lattice-topped flan.

INGREDIENTS

- 400g sweet shortcrust pastry (see page 32)
- Small handful of stem ginger drained and chopped (or you could use crystallised)
- Small handful of stoneless dates chopped
- 40g caster sugar
- 40g butter
- 2 – aw go on, make it 3 – tablespoons of dark rum
- 1 egg beaten

METHOD

1 First make the pastry case. Preheat the oven to 200°C. Make the sweet shortcrust pastry as described on page 32 and chill for 30 minutes. Cut off a quarter to make the lattice strips. Roll the rest out to the thickness of a pound coin, prick with a fork and line your tin with it. Blind bake for 15 minutes until the pastry is a pale golden colour. Let it cool down (but leave in the tin). Turn oven down to 160°C.

2 In a bowl, cream the butter and sugar together with the rum, and add the dates. Pour the mix into the pastry case. Roll out the remaining pastry and, using a ruler and a pizza wheel (or a knife if you've got steady hands), make your lattice strips. Dust with some flour to stop them sticking.

3 Brush the edge of the pastry case with the beaten egg and lay your strips on, weaving them under and over each other. It's a bit fiddly, this, but take it slow and steady. Alternatively do the weaving on a sheet of greaseproof paper, place another piece of paper on top of the finished lattice, and quickly invert and slide over the top of your pie.

4 Crimp any lattice strips that join the edge of the pie and brush the top with beaten egg.

5 Bake in the oven for about 20–25 minutes at 160° until the pastry is golden brown. Leave to cool a little before serving.

Pecan pie

A modern American classic, and often eaten at Thanksgiving and Christmas. Many US recipes call for corn syrup, which might be tricky to track down in the UK, so use maple or golden syrup instead if you have to.

INGREDIENTS

- 100g muscovado sugar
- 2 tablespoons of maple or golden syrup
- 100g butter
- 3 eggs beaten
- 300g pecan nuts chopped
- Handful of whole pecans for decoration
- 400g sweet shortcrust pastry (see page 32)

METHOD

1 Make the sweet shortcrust pastry by putting the flour and sugar in a bowl and rubbing in the fat. Add a little water and combine to form a dough. Bring together and squash into a lozenge shape, wrap in cling film and chill. Alternatively make it in a food processor or use ready-made. Get your oven up to 180°C.

2 Roll it out to the thickness of a pound coin, line your tin with it and prick with a fork. Blind bake for 15 minutes until the pastry is a pale golden colour. Remove the paper. Let it cool (but leave it in the tin).

3 In a bowl, mix the eggs, syrup and sugar. Melt the butter in a pan and slowly add to the eggy sugar mixture, whisking all the time. Add the chopped pecans and pour into the pastry case.

4 Bake for 40–50 minutes at 160°C until the pastry is golden and the filling set. Leave to cool a little before removing from the tin. Can be served warm or cold.

Lemon meringue pie

Fluffy, cloud-like meringue on top; sharp, golden, lemony filling; and a firm biscuity pastry base, lemon meringue is a classic. It's also rather a refreshing and cooling pudding. Cornflour ensures your lemon mixture sets – there are some recipes that don't use it, but that's taking a gamble in my opinion. Also, the lemon mixture should give a good thwack of lemon in the mouth, not be bland yellow jam. The lemon layer contrasts the sweeter meringue above it.

INGREDIENTS

For the filling
- 4 tablespoons of cornflour
- 100g golden caster sugar
- Juice and grated zest of 4 unwaxed lemons
- 50g butter cut into pieces
- 3 egg yolks and 1 whole egg
- 1 egg yolk beaten
- 5 egg whites
- 100ml water
- 400g sweet shortcrust pastry (page 32)
- 100g icing sugar
- 100g caster sugar

A word on the amount of eggs in the recipe: you'll end up with one egg yolk left over, but you can beat it and freeze it.

METHOD

To make the pastry case
1 Preheat the oven to 200°C.
2 Make the sweet shortcrust pastry as described on page 32 and chill for 30 minutes.
3 Roll it out to the thickness of a pound coin, prick with a fork and line your tin with it.
4 Blind bake for 15 minutes until the pastry is a pale golden colour. Remove the paper and brush with the one beaten egg yolk. This should form a barrier between your filling and the pastry. Let cool (but leave it in the tin). Turn oven down to 180°C.

To make the filling
5 Add the cornflour to the cold water, then the lemon juice, grated zest and sugar, and place in a pan on a low heat stirring all the time, first with a spoon then later a whisk – don't let it boil.
6 When it's begun to thicken, add the softened butter one piece at a time.
7 Add the 3 egg yolks and 1 whole egg beaten together, and continue to whisk over a low heat until thickened. Allow to cool. When cool, pour into the pastry case.

To make the meringue
8 First make sure your bowl and beaters are spotlessly clean.
9 Take the egg whites, put in a bowl and whisk until you get soft peaks. Gradually add the caster sugar.
10 Gently spread the meringue over the lemon layer and bake in the oven until the meringue is a light golden brown (around 40 minutes). You can pipe it if you have a piping bag and want to get fancy.
11 Leave to cool before serving.

Banoffee pie

Banoffee pie was invented at the Hungry Monk Restaurant in Polegate, East Sussex, in 1972 by Ian Dowding. A chance conversation with his sister about boiling unopened cans of condensed milk led him to create a soft, toffee-like sauce to which he added bananas. Alas, the restaurant has now closed, but here, by kind permission, is the original Banoffee pie recipe as it first appeared in *The Deeper Secrets of the Hungry Monk* book, published in 1974. This will serve eight to ten people.

INGREDIENTS
- 340g sweet shortcrust pastry (page 32)
- 1.5 tins condensed milk (13.5oz each)
- 680g firm bananas
- 375ml double cream
- Half a teaspoon of powdered instant coffee
- 1 dessertspoon of caster sugar
- A little freshly ground coffee

METHOD
1 Preheat the oven to 190°C. Lightly grease a 10in x 1.5in (25cm x 4cm) flan tin. Line this with the pastry, thinly rolled out. Prick the base all over with a fork and bake blind until crisp. Allow to cool.
2 The secret of this delicious pudding lies in the condensed milk. Immerse the cans unopened in a deep pan of boiling water. Cover and boil for 3 hours, making sure that the pan doesn't boil dry.

3 Remove the tin from the water and allow to cool completely before opening. Inside you will find the soft toffee filling.
4 Whip the cream with the instant coffee and sugar until thick and smooth. Now spread the toffee over the base of the flan.
5 Peel and halve the bananas lengthways and lay them on the toffee. Finally, spoon or pipe on the cream and lightly sprinkle the freshly ground coffee over it.

Caution
It is absolutely vital to top up the pan of boiling water frequently during the cooking of the cans. Three hours is a long time, and if they're allowed to boil dry the cans will explode, presenting a grave risk to life, limb and kitchen ceilings.

Hint
Banoffee is a marvellous 'emergency' pudding once you have the toffee mixture in your store cupboard. We therefore suggest that you boil several cans at the same time, as they keep unopened indefinitely.

Tart Tatin

There's always a story attached to how dishes came to be invented, and you can rest assured that mishap and error aren't far behind. So it is with tart Tatin, apparently introduced to the world by the Tatin sisters in their hotel in France when an apple pie somehow went wrong and they flipped it out of the dish and tried to pass it off as OK. Well, you would, wouldn't you? Lo and behold, everyone loved it, rather than saying 'What the hell's this mess?', and the rest is history. You can Tatin anything, really, tomatoes (page 133) and sausages (page 141), for instance; and you can use pears or plums instead of apples, and bananas and rum would be a nice combination too. You'll need a small ovenproof frying pan (20cm) for this.

INGREDIENTS

- 160g ready-made puff pastry
- 100g butter
- 10ml water
- 100g caster sugar
- 8 Cox's apples peeled, cored and halved

METHOD

1 Prepare the apples. (You can do this a day ahead and store them in the fridge. They'll turn brown, but they're going to get caramelised anyway.)

2 Put the butter, water and sugar in the pan on a high heat until the sugar starts to melt and go golden brown. You're after a caramel. Turn the heat down and add the apple halves. You may need to break a few up to fill in the gaps.

3 Preheat the oven to 200°C.

4 Roll out the pastry to about 0.5cm thick and, using a small plate just a bit bigger than your pan, cut a round disc. Place this on top of the apples and tuck the edges down inside the pan. Cook for 25–30 minutes until the pastry has risen, then leave to cool for five minutes. Carefully invert on to a plate and serve, still warm, with some cream.

Apple crumble

There's an interesting history to the apple crumble. Many people assume it's some olde worlde recipe handed down through the centuries. Actually it's not that old. During World War Two many of the ingredients to make pastry – butter, sugar and flour – were rationed. Without them, making an apple pie (page 150) was tricky. So what little ingredients they had were instead used to make a topping. Once the butter was gone, other fats were used, and oats could be added to bulk out the flour. Everyone loves apple crumble, and it's one of the easiest recipes to make in this book.

INGREDIENTS

For the topping
- 130g plain flour
- 50g oats
- 100g muscovado or dark brown sugar
- 80g unsalted butter chopped into small pieces

For the filling
- 4–6 cooking apples
- Pinch of cinnamon or nutmeg
- Teaspoon of water

The key to a good crumble is to ensure you get a good crunchy topping on top, but slightly gooey and stewy apple underneath. Too much flour and not enough fat and that won't happen. Sugar in the topping also plays a crucial roll in providing crunch and sweetness. I think the darker and more molasses-like the better.

Crumble should be about the yin and yang interplay between the soft but tart filling and sweet but crunchy topping, therefore I tend to avoid adding sugar to the filling, given that there's already plenty in the topping and the custard. However, if you're making this for kids or you've a particularly sweet tooth, add 30g or so to the stewed apples.

This recipe fills an oblong dish about 25cm x 15cm and 4cm deep.

METHOD

1 Peel and core your apples and chop into chunks. Place in a saucepan, add a pinch of cinnamon, a dribble of water or apple juice, and put on a low heat for 15 minutes. When the apples start to break down, remove and leave to cool.

2 Make your topping by combining flour, oats, spices and sugar in a bowl and rubbing in the butter. It should be a sandy colour. Spoon the mixture over the cooled apple mix and bake in the oven for 30 minutes at 170°C until the top looks golden and brown.

3 Serve with custard, ice cream, cream or all three.

Alternative method

Too much rubbing in of the butter will start to melt it, so this recipe is an ideal one to try out the grated frozen butter technique. Freeze the butter and then grate into the flour, combine quickly and top the apple mix.

Rhubarb and stem ginger pie

I love rhubarb, and what's more it's really good for you. Helps with your bladder or something. As it's originally from China (indeed, so is the apple come to think of it) I've paired it with crystallised ginger, which gives the pie a real fiery kick! You can find crystallised ginger in most supermarkets.

INGREDIENTS

- 600g sweet shortcrust pastry
- 500g rhubarb washed and cut into 2cm/1in lengths
- 150g golden caster sugar
- 10 chunks of crystallised stem ginger chopped
- 1 egg beaten

METHOD

1 First make the pastry case. Preheat the oven to 200°C. Make the sweet shortcrust pastry as described on page 32 and chill for 30 minutes. Remove a bit more than a third and return it to the fridge. Roll out the remainder to the thickness of a pound coin, prick with a fork, and line your tin with it.

2 Blind bake for 15 minutes until the pastry is a light, pale, golden colour. Remove the paper and brush the pastry with the one beaten egg yolk – this should form a barrier between the filling and the pastry – and return to the oven for a few moments.

3 When the egg layer is cooked, trim off the overhanging edges and let the case cool (but leave it in the tin).

4 Mix the prepared rhubarb in a bowl with the ginger and the sugar until coated. Transfer to the blind-baked case. Roll out the remaining pastry from the fridge to form the lid. Brush the edge with the beaten egg, and place the lid on top. Crimp together around the edge and make a small hole in the centre to let out any steam. Brush with the remaining egg and dust with some more caster sugar.

5 Bake in the oven at 200°C for around 30 minutes until pastry is golden brown.

Pear and chocolate chip pie

One to make if you happen on a windfall of fresh, really ripe pears. You'll need around eight to ten depending on size, otherwise you can use tinned – drain them well, though, as they'll be a lot wetter. This pie is a double crust, but you could make it as a crumble. You could also add other dried fruits, some booze or even, wait for it, some cheese (take out the chocolate if you're going to do that, though).

INGREDIENTS

- 8–10 pears peeled, cored and sliced into quarters
- Handful of chocolate chips
- 50g butter cut into small cubes
- 40g caster sugar
- 1 egg beaten
- 600g sweet shortcrust pastry (page 32)

METHOD

1 First make the pastry case. Preheat the oven to 200°C. Make the sweet shortcrust pastry as described on page 32 and chill for 30 minutes. Remove a bit more than a third and return it to the fridge. Roll out the remainder to the thickness of a pound coin, prick with a fork, and line your tin with it.

2 Blind bake for 15 minutes until the pastry is a light, pale, golden colour. Remove the paper and brush the pastry with the one beaten egg yolk – this should form a barrier between the filling and the pastry – and return to the oven for a few moments.

3 When the egg layer is cooked, trim off the overhanging edges and let the case cool (but leave it in the tin).

4 Arrange the pieces of pear in the pastry case in a circular design, dot with the butter and sprinkle with the chocolate chips.

5 Roll out the remaining pastry from the fridge to form a lid. Brush the edge of the pastry case containing the filling with egg wash, and place the lid on top. Cut a small hole to let out any steam. Crimp the edges and brush the top with the remainder of the egg wash. Sprinkle with a bit more caster sugar and bake in a hot oven (180°C) for about 30 minutes until the pastry in cooked and golden brown.

Gooseberry pie

Gooseberries are ace, but we don't see enough of them in the shops these days. You often see them paired with mackerel in recipes, where their sharpness counters the fish's naturally fattiness. Here I've used them in a classic pie. This makes a double-crust in a round 18cm pie tin.

INGREDIENTS

- 600g sweet shortcrust pastry (page 32)
- 800g gooseberries with the little tip bit picked off
- 150g caster sugar, plus a bit extra for dusting
- Glug of elderflower cordial
- 2 tablespoons of cornflour
- 1 egg beaten

METHOD

1 First make the pastry case. Preheat the oven to 200°C. Make the sweet shortcrust pastry as described on page 32 and chill for 30 minutes. Remove a bit more than a third and return it to the fridge. Roll out the remainder to the thickness of a pound coin, prick with a fork, and line your tin with it.

2 Blind bake for 15 minutes until the pastry is a light, pale, golden colour. Remove the paper and brush the pastry with the one beaten egg yolk – this should form a barrier between the filling and the pastry – and return to the oven for a few moments.

3 When the egg layer is cooked, trim off the overhanging edges and let the case cool (but leave it in the tin).

4 Wash the gooseberries and put half of them in a pan with the sugar, elderflower cordial and cornflour. Simmer and stir until the gooseberries have broken down and the mixture has thickened. Add the remaining gooseberries to soften a little and leave to cool.

5 Spoon the cooled filling into the pastry case and roll out the remaining pastry from the fridge to form the lid. Brush the edge with the beaten egg, and place the lid on top. Crimp together around the edge and make a small hole in the centre to let out any steam. Brush with the remaining egg and dust over some more caster sugar.

6 Bake in the oven at 200°C for around 30 minutes until the pastry is golden brown. Serve warm rather than hot, with ice cream, cream or custard.

CHAPTER 11

ACCOMPANIMENTS

You've done it! Through hard work, skill and sheer bloody-mindedness you've achieved the perfect balance of pastry, filling and sauce. You've made a pie! Well done, mate.

The kitchen may look like a bomb's hit it, and there's probably a fair bit of washing up, but you don't care, because you and you alone (until your friends or family arrive) are looking at a warm, golden pie, and can say 'I made that'.

Now, you could just plough right in – after all, you've earned it. But there are a few little extras, sauces and side dishes that you might want to consider serving with your pie. Firstly there's condiments, long-lasting cold sauces that come ready-made in bottles; next there are sauces, custard and gravy, which are best made yourself and eaten there and then. And finally there's relishes and pickles; these can be either homemade or bought, and come in jars.

Just as tomatoes need a little seasoning of salt to bring out their flavour, pies do benefit from a blob, dribble or dollop of something punchy to help take the flavour up to 11, by providing a counterpoint in flavour and texture to the pie itself.

How to make proper mashed potatoes

By no stretch of the imagination can you call mashed potatoes a condiment, sauce or relish, but I've included them here because they're a popular side to serve with pie, and not just in Cockney pie'n'mash shops either.

INGREDIENTS

- 6 large potatoes
- 20g butter at room temperature
- Splash of milk
- Pinch of salt

Leftovers

You should always make too much mash. Leftovers can be mixed with any vegetables and used in my bubble and squeak pie (page 129). Or if you want to get fancy you could make Duchess potatoes: spoon the cold mash into a piping bag and pipe it into little cones before transferring to a hot oven to brown.

There's something about the soft, fluffy butteriness of mash that's just perfect with a pie, and I'm not quite sure why that is. They just *work*. Roast potatoes just don't feel right with pie – their lot is with a roast dinner. I don't think chips really shine served next to pie either.

So, pie and mash is the perfect combination, and here's how to make utterly perfect mash time after time with pretty much any spud. The secret, gentlemen, is ... buy a potato ricer. These handy contraptions squeeze the cooked potatoes through tiny holes into little strands that fall into the waiting bowl. They make making mash a doddle – far easier than all that pounding with a potato masher that the Smash robots found so amusing in the 1970s.

Remember, mash isn't just a side, it's 'part of' dishes like shepherd's pie (page 116) and cottage pie (page 119). But while the mash for those dishes goes back in the oven, allowing any lumpy bits to cook out, mash served straight up is afforded no such luxury. As such, it's got to be top notch.

THE BEST SPUDS

Maris Piper are the universally acknowledged spuds, and they're good, but a bit ... well, pedestrian. By all means use them, but keep an eye out for other floury dry varieties out there that'll work just as well, if not better. Try to find Mozart, Vivaldi, Rooster, Saxon and hot young newcomer on the culinary potato scene Vales Sovereign.

The following recipe serves four, with some left over. Basically you need to allow one large potato or two small ones per person.

METHOD

1 Peel and quarter the potatoes.
2 Place in a large pan of cold water and bring to the boil.
3 Turn down to a gentle rolling boil. You don't want to fast boil potatoes, like you might pasta.
4 After about 15–20 minutes poke a skewer or small knife into the centre of the largest spud. If it gives easily, they're probably done.
5 Remove and drain, then leave in the colander for 10 minutes. This step is very important – right now those potatoes are soaking wet, and they need time to dry out. Mashing them now will give you watery mash. Instead, wait until you can see little white dry bits on the edges.
6 Place each quarter into your potato ricer and squeeze into the pan. Add a huge knob of butter, dash of milk or cream, and gently mix together. I promise you, it'll be mash worthy of a place next to your pie.

ADDITIONS TO MASHED POTATO

Garlic is a great addition to mashed potatoes. Peel 4 or 5 cloves and infuse in melted butter on the lowest heat your hob will do.

There's a French dish called *aligot* which sees garlic, milk and cheese added to mashed potatoes, which are then beaten until they almost become as stretchy as a fondue. Nice, but perhaps not a good accompaniment to pie.

More butter

The French chef Joel Robuchon is famous for using half as much butter as potato in his recipe. He also cooks his potatoes in their skins, then peels them once they're cool enough to handle.

Cheese

Cheesy mash is ace, isn't it? You'll need something with a strongish flavour – a good Cheddar, or one of the nuttier Northern European cheeses. Simply grate and mix in.

Herbs

Herbs can be added to mash. Adding spring onion makes the Irish dish called 'champ', while added cabbage or kale makes 'colcannon'. Both would be good with the beef and Guinness cobbler on page 123.

Making proper gravy

There's much debate about gravy. Rather than a light, clear, flavourful sauce to anoint our meat or pies, it seems we've been conditioned over the years so that many people actually prefer opaque, thick-as-gloss-paint, gloopy gravy these days. Well, I'm here to tell you that's wrong. Gravy is a sauce, it isn't brown custard.

INGREDIENTS

- 500ml stock
- 1 teaspoon of plain flour
- 1 tablespoon of water
- Salt and pepper

Gravy granules may save time, but I think they taste horrible and contain little more than starch, a caramel brown food colouring (E150C) and salt. To paraphrase the old nautical saying, you don't want to spoil the pie for a ha'porth of gravy. What's the point of going to all the effort of making a lovely homemade pie, only to smother its wonderful flavours in 'edible creosote'? None, I say.

'What about gravy browning?' you ask. Well, that's a complete waste of money too. It basically consists of our old friend E150C, salt and glucose.

You know your lovely stocks you made back in chapter 3? They're the key to good gravy. Just take one out of the freezer, pop it in a small saucepan and heat up.

The recipe here will serve four people.

METHOD

Thickening gravy

Gravy will thicken by itself as it reduces. The downside with this is that as it does so it reduces the amount of gravy you have left to serve. Fine for one or two, but not enough to go round a table crammed with extended family for Sunday lunch. You could double up the amount, or use a small amount of plain flour to thicken your stock so as to keep the volume. Don't put the flour straight into the hot gravy, however – it'll just turn to lumps and ruin it. Instead put a teaspoon of the flour in a teacup and add a tablespoon of cold water.

Mix this together until the flour is dissolved. It should look like thin cream. Now add one teaspoon of this mixture to your gravy and stir. It'll take a few moments to cook and start to thicken your sauce – you'll need to bring it up to the boil then down to a simmer. It may be that one teaspoon is enough, but if it's not add another teaspoon. Judge by eye and remember to taste it – if it tastes powdery, you need to cook out the flour a bit more.

WHAT ABOUT CORNFLOUR?

Saint Delia of Norwich says cornflour gives a gloopy texture, and if you use too much it will. It's much 'stronger' than plain flour, so you need much less. Cornflour is best used to thicken your sauce inside the pie, rather than to thicken the gravy.

SEASONING

Remember, we didn't add salt to the stock when making it, so now's the time to check the seasoning for your gravy. A couple of twists of pepper and a pinch of salt at the end will see it right.

Pies don't need to be served with as much gravy as, say, a roast dinner. You're just after a little something extra to moisten, say, the mash, or roast potatoes.

Additional flavours

Serving separate gravy lets you add additional flavours that will complement your pie. Here are some popular ones:

- **Red wine** – a glug of red wine in your stock will add a richer note; the booze will cook out. Let it reduce for a bit longer, and go easy on any other thickenings. Best for beef dishes.
- **White wine** – as above, best served with things like chicken or vegetable pies.
- **Other booze** – port, beer, cider and masala can all be added too. I'd steer clear of lager, spirits and alcopops, mind.
- **Redcurrant jelly** – this adds a sharper citrus note to gravy.
- **Mustard** – a teaspoon of Dijon mustard gives gravy a real kick. Works best with pork-based pies.
- **Onions** – onion gravy is great, but you need to chop the onions finely into small pieces, and sweat them right down – I'm talking 30 minutes or more – on a very, very low heat, before adding your frozen stock. Adding a pinch of salt draws out the moisture and will help them break down faster; you consequently don't need to season at the end. Some finally chopped garlic wouldn't hurt either.

ANOTHER WAY TO MAKE GRAVY

If you do want a thicker, more opaque gravy, don't reach for the gravy granules. Make a roux (page 52), but instead of adding milk add your stock. This will produce a very light tan-coloured gravy, what I call 'American' gravy. Goes particularly well with turkey.

A WORD ABOUT GRAVY BOATS

In times past, to pour gravy directly on to your food from the sauce boat would have marked you out as uncouth. Sauce boats always came with a spoon or ladle that allowed you, or more likely the servant waiting on you, to ladle one or two spoons of sauce over your food. The spout on a sauce boat was where the ladle rested.

Somewhere between the end of WW1 and the invention of Bisto the gravy spoon went missing in the cutlery drawer of history, but if you want the full Downton experience buy a sauce spoon for your gravy boat. It's the *proper* way to do it.

Ketchups and condiments

TOMATO KETCHUP

To be honest, it's a sauce for children. If you're a grown man and still slathering everything with the sugary red stuff, you need to have a word with yourself. It doesn't have any redeeming features when paired with pie in my book (and this is *my* book). Save it for the nippers...

BROWN SAUCE

This is an entirely different beast: robust, sweet yes but also sharp and spicy, tangy almost, piquant. Brown sauce is the legacy of Britain's Victorian Empire condensed into one bottle.

For my money, brown sauce works best with cold pies, particularly pork. You need its oomph to contrast the rich fatty flavours and jelly. I can, however, take a blob on a hot pie. I don't think it does chicken or any of the lighter pies any favours. A raised game pie can handle it, though.

MUSTARD

A condiment that really separates the men from the boys. Mustard was the traditional foil of roast beef, consequently any beef pie can take it on. English mustard tends to be the hottest, with a vivid yellow colour; then there's the more effete French versions, like Dijon. Mustard also works with pork.

HORSERADISH

This has stolen the lead over mustard as the go-to condiment for beef, and while that works for roast meats I don't think horseradish works that well when served with a pie. Still, give it a go, and see what you think.

MINT SAUCE

Normally served with lamb, so there's no reason why it can't be served with lamb in pies.

CUMBERLAND SAUCE

Made from port, redcurrant jelly and the zest of oranges and lemons, with a blob of mustard and ginger thrown in for good measure. This classic sauce – always served cold – accompanies meats such as gammon, goose and tongue. Where it really comes into its own, however, is with game.

To make it zesty cut the citrus fruits into very thin strips, then blanch to remove any bitterness. Mix the port and redcurrant jelly over a low heat, add a teaspoon of mustard and pinch of ground ginger, season, leave to cool and serve.

Piccalilli and relishes

PICCALILLI

Whether on the picnic blanket or the Christmas table, this classic British accompaniment to cheese, cold meats and pork pies is a real all-rounder. It's also really easy to make your own. Making piccalilli is one of those autumnal jobs that's actually fun, unlike checking the hot water system and clearing your gutters of leaves. Cauliflower, cucumber, courgettes, runner or green beans are all fair game for a right good 'lillin'. You could add a bit of chopped peppers for colour, silver skin onions, maybe some chilli if you want an extra, different kind of heat.

Key things are the right balance of vinegars against some sugar, and lots of mustard and turmeric to get that vivid yellow colour. I once skimped on the latter and my pickle looked like sick.

PARSLEY LIQUOR

The Cockney's sauce found in pie and mash shops used to be made with the juice from stewed eels, flecked green with parsley, but these days it's more likely to be made without it. It's easy to make at home. Make a roux (page 52) and thin down with water or chicken stock until smooth. A tablespoon of white wine vinegar adds a bit of bite. Add the parsley and cook for a few more minutes before serving.

ONION MARMALADE

This sweet, brown, sticky onion sauce was revived from an old historic recipe by Tracklements in Wiltshire. It's fantastic with cold pies. A spoon or two in your gravy should help it along no end too. Brays Cottage Pork Pies (www.perfectpie.co.uk) actually use it in the pies themselves. You can make it yourself, but it takes a hell of a lot of onions and long, slow cooking to render them down to that brown sticky caramel stage.

Sauce ravigote

This is my tweaked version of the classic French sauce ravigote. It goes really well with milder chicken pies such as chicken and fennel pie (page 93). It should be punchy (*ravigoté* means 'rejuvenated') in the mouth and provide a contrast to the chicken, though it works with salmon and rabbit pretty well too. You could add a teaspoon of Dijon mustard if you wanted extra bite.

INGREDIENTS
- 2 tablespoons of chopped capers
- 2 tablespoons of chopped baby gherkins
- 1 tablespoon of chopped parsley
- 1 tablespoon of chopped tarragon (or big pinch of dried)
- One garlic clove grated
- Good glug of olive oil
- Salt and pepper

METHOD
1 Chop everything as finely as you can be bothered.
2 Combine together about 40 minutes before you need it, to give the flavours time to mingle.

Mushy peas, pickled red cabbage

PEAS

The humble green pea, that tiny little piece of summer, loves to buddy up to a good pie. Rather than snatching them from the freezer and then boiling the bejeezus out of them, let them defrost, then cook them gently in a frying pan with a big knob of butter and a little water with a good pinch of salt and pepper. They'll taste better, stay warmer longer and won't do that weird shrivelling thing that makes them look like little hexagons.

MUSHY PEAS

If you're not from the Midlands or the North of England, you probably don't really understand mushy peas. I've been in chip shops in the South that don't even offer them, a situation eloquently summed up by the Bard of Bolton Peter Kay's line 'Has tha nowt moist?'

Proper mushy peas are made from marrowfat peas and are neon green thanks to the addition of Brilliant Blue FCF (E133, a dye made from coal tar) and Tartrazine (E102, a synthetic man-made yellow dye) – yum! The result should be thick enough to grout a bathroom.

And please avoid flavour trespassers such as mint, Greek yoghurt and lemon juice that have been applied to the humble pea to make something called a pea purée. This, one imagines, is an attempt to drag mushy peas upmarket but is, in my eyes, a betrayal of class and region. Incidentally, the tale about Peter Mandelson mistaking mushy peas for guacamole isn't true.

Pea-wet, rarely seen nowadays, is the juice left over from making mushy peas.

RED CABBAGE

Red cabbage, cooked for the best part of a day with red wine vinegar, spices and brown sugar, is a great side dish for game and festive pies. The pickled version's good too, particularly with cold pies. Pickled red cabbage is a traditional accompaniment to scouse, the Liverpudlian meat stew that gives Scousers their name. And after all, like a lad out on the town without a jacket, scouse is but a pie that's gone out without its pastry.

Baked beans

INGREDIENTS

- 1 medium onion
- 3 cans of any white beans (Borlotti, navy beans etc)
- 1 tin of chopped tomatoes
- 1 tablespoon of black treacle
- 1 large teaspoon of Tabasco or Cholula Hot Sauce
- ½ teaspoon of mild chilli powder
- Salt and pepper

I think beans *and* pie is too much brown carbs on the plate, to be honest, especially if spuds are there too – what are you, a weightlifter? Pies need something green, fresh and punchy to cut against them.

However, you're entitled to think otherwise. With that in mind, here's my recipe to make some amazing baked beans.

METHOD

1 Chop the onion and fry in an ovenproof casserole until golden.
2 Add the drained tins of beans and all other ingredients and combine.
3 Put in a low oven (around 140°C) for 4 or 5 hours.

Beer

You will, I'm sure, feel that beer is a good accompaniment to most things in life, and pie is no exception. There are some truly excellent modern craft beers being produced nowadays, that cut against generic 5.2% fizzy lagers all owned by the same multinational juggernaut, and rather boring Real Ale 'session' beers. ('Session beer' is such a stupid term, isn't it? You don't see 'session wine', do you?)

NO RULES, JUST SOME HARD-LEARNED ADVICE

Now a pie's a pretty substantial meal, and I don't think you want to fill up on too much liquid. No, here we must look to stronger flavoursome beers – from both home and abroad – that offer strength and flavour to enhance the enjoyment of our pie, rather than quantity.

I take it you'll be eating your pie at home, having made it yourself, so that rules out cask ale from a pub (unless you live near one and can carry it home). Let's look instead to bottled beer. Your average large supermarket now stocks a range of ales and beers to explore, but do try and find a vintners or good off-licence, as they'll have some real gems, such as:

- **Kernel Brewery** – brewed in South London, and only available in selected independent retailers. They produce a range of beers, with the IPA a good place to start.
- **Meantime Brewery** – their Chocolate porter is my 'go to' beer for the beef and ale pie (page 63), and you could continue the theme by serving it with the dish.
- **BrewDog** – the bad boys of beer making, they brew all sorts of interesting and complex beers. Widely available.
- **Your regional or local brewery** – chances are there's someone in your town, district or region who's making real ale. Do try and support their efforts.

The bigger players, like Adnams from Suffolk and Sharp's from Cornwall, produce consistently good beers that are widely available. Look out for Adnams' seasonal brews, particularly the Tally Ho!

STOUTS

Stouts and porters are dark, complex beers, yet despite this they're often served with oysters. They're great with the richer beef dishes too.

CIDER

As a lad growing up, cider was horrible chemical fizzy stuff, used only in snakebite. Now there's loads of really good cider available from all over the country. Naturally it works best with pies containing pork and sausage, but it also goes quite happily with sweeter pies, particularly those containing apple. Don't forget perry either.

WINE

I'm not that big a fan of adding wine to pie fillings (some chicken pies being a notable exception). I think beer works better, particularly for red-meat-based pies. It's less sharp, and you also get a much bigger range of flavours and styles with beer than with wine. I am, however, a fan of drinking the stuff, and red wine with red meat, white wine with chicken and fish, is the orthodox mantra, and is generally true. Well, not always. A light pinot noir can swing both ways, though it's a bit out of its depth when on the table with some of the stronger beef and games dishes. For those you must look to rich, strong reds.

SPIRITS

I prefer a wee dram after eating rather than with food. But if you do want to pair whiskies with pies, you're better off looking to the more full-bodied varieties aged in sherry casks.

How to make proper custard

Custard, a sauce so British that even the French call it *crème anglaise*, is the oil in the engine for the staple British pudding. It's our contribution to the world of dessert accompaniments. If you're making apple pie (page 150) you've *got* to have custard. Crème is just custard that hasn't got itself together yet, while ice cream is just a frozen custard.

INGREDIENTS

- 300ml full fat milk
- 3 egg yolks
- 4 tablespoons of caster sugar
- 1 vanilla pod or teaspoon of vanilla extract (optional)

A POTTED HISTORY OF BIRD'S CUSTARD POWDER

Growing up in the '70s custard meant one thing: the magic yellow powder that was Bird's, made in, and served out of, an old Pyrex jug. Alfred Bird invented his eponymous powder in 1837 as his wife was allergic to eggs. Yes, that's right, it doesn't contain any, just annatto – a yellow colour made from a South American nut – and cornflour. To this you added hot milk and sugar, giving the sweet, bright, yellow sauce.

Today, of course, reaching into the chiller cabinet you can grab a pot of single estate Madagascan vanilla custard made with free-range eggs and Fairtrade golden caster sugar, for under £2 – oh, how far we've come.

Making your own custard is dead easy, though. If you've got two eggs and some milk and sugar, you're laughing.

METHOD

1 Put the milk in a pan, add the vanilla pod if using and bring up to a boil. Set aside and let the pod infuse in the milk. After 20 minutes remove the pod, and set aside to dry.

2 Whisk the eggs for a minute or two, then add the caster sugar and whisk for another 2–3 minutes until light yellow and fluffy. Add a small amount of the warm milk and mix gently. Add the egg mix back to the warm milk and return to the hob on a low heat.

3 Keep stirring and after a few minutes the sauce will thicken. Serve straight away or keep on one side with a lid on to stop a skin forming.

THAT VANILLA POD

Vanilla pods aren't cheap, but they can be used three or four times. Another top tip is to put the pod in a sealed jar of caster sugar. The sugar takes on the flavour of the vanilla and can be used in the next custard you make.

EXTRA INGREDIENTS

Though we all think vanilla is the traditional flavouring in custard, history says otherwise. There are many older recipes that add things like cinnamon, lemon peel, brandy and peach water to increase the flavouring.

CHAPTER 12
PIES I HAVE KNOWN

THE MASSIVE BRITISH-SHAPED PORK PIE

It started with the dish. Around the time of William and Kate's wedding, every shop in the land was chock-a-block with Union Jack this and British-themed that. Amongst the tea towels and biscuit tins, however, there was one item that caught my eye. The Brit-bowl, a dish shaped like Britain, which I found in the Adnams shop in Southwold, Suffolk.

As soon as I saw it I knew I wanted to make a pie in it, and called in some pastry support in the form of Sarah Petigree, owner of Bray's Cottage pies (www.perfectpie.co.uk). For something this size and weight we were always going to need the structural rigidity of a hot-water crust, only this time Sarah and I upped the strong bread flour content.

The pastry was carefully moulded around the coastline of the dish, and Sarah's unique filling of pork, smoked bacon and secret blend of spices was judiciously applied, first to the West Country, then the South-East, the Midlands, Wales, the North and finally Scotland.

The top went on and 'Pie Britannia' was slid into a hot oven: 45 minutes later it was ready. It took a day to cool down, but once it did it came out of the dish with remarkable ease. I still can't believe it worked, but there you have it, a foot-long pork pie in the shape of Britain. What's not to like?

THE HISTORY OF DENBY DALE PIE

They know a thing or two about pies in Denby, West Yorkshire. The town is famous in pie circles for baking huge pies to celebrate national events.

The first giant pie was baked in 1788 to celebrate George III becoming – if only for a short time – a little less mad. The second great pie celebrated the Duke of Wellington's victory at Waterloo in 1815. The first slice was cut by local soldier George Wilby, who fought in the battle.

Thirty one years later a pie was again baked for the repealing of the corn laws (those Victorians were party animals!). No one got to eat this pie, however, as the stage holding it collapsed as the crowd stampeded to get a portion. There were rumours of sabotage by villagers from nearby Clayton West.

Queen Victoria celebrated her Golden Jubilee in 1887, and in a fit of Royal fervour a *huge* pie over eight feet wide was planned. The filling contained 1,581lb of beef, 163lb of veal, 180lb of lamb, 180lb of mutton, 250lb of lean pork, 67 rabbits and hares and 153 various game birds and poultry. However, disaster again struck when it turned out the game birds weren't so much 'high' as rotten, and the whole pie stank. It was taken to the woods and buried.

In the 20th century more pies were made celebrating victory in World War One, bicentennials and Royal births. The last Denby Dale to date was baked to celebrate the Millennium, and was 12m long, 2.5m wide and 1m deep. As for when the next one will be, who knows? They tend to come about every 25 years, so let's hope there's a significant national event around 2025.

THE DWARF IN A PYE

In the 16th century, Royal chefs would place live animals like birds in a pie, so that 'when the pie was opened, the birds began to sing', as the old nursery rhyme goes.

With the invention of the DVD boxed set still 400 years away, pies – and indeed many other foods at large banquets – were often part of the entertainment. Woe betide the host who didn't lay on amusement and wonder as part of the feast. By the 1620s, however, live song birds in a pie was becoming a bit 'meh'. So when George Villiers, Duke of Buckingham, hosted King Charles I and his grumpy new teen bride Henrietta Maria of France, he pulled out all the stops in an attempt to win favour.

Towards the end of the feast a large pie was presented to the Queen and she was invited to carve it. Before she could do so, however, the pastry began to crack, and out came a tiny hand, then an arm and a helmet, until all 18in of the seven-year-old Jeffery Hudson stood on the table. Lacking the correct growth hormone, Jeffery never grew much taller than 3ft, but as a child he was tiny.

History does not relate what exactly he said or did as he sprang from the pie, but one might imagine him making a short speech, or marching up and down.

This, then, was the ultimate pie as spectacle and theatre, and crucially for Buckingham it cemented his place (for a short while at least) at the King's side.

The teenage Queen, who surrounded herself with small animals, took the dwarf as a gift, perhaps more a living doll. Jeffery went on to have one of the most remarkable lives in history, privy to the great people and events of the age. He fought for the King at the Battle of Worcester, escaped to France, killed in a duel someone who made fun of his height, was exiled, and was captured by pirates and forced into slavery in North Africa for 25 years before being ransomed and making his way back to England, only to die penniless. And it all started with a pie.

THE DARTH VADER PIE

A quick browse of any online cookery equipment store reveals a host of novelty cake tins for baking cakes. However, you can also use these to make pies. After all, a tin is a tin, right?

Here I've used the chilling face mask of the Dark Lord of the Sith himself as a mould, with the filling from the beef and Guinness cobbler (page 123), but you could use any filling you fancied. For the full Star Wars meal experience serve with pak choi and Aunt Beru's famous blue milk. However, if you wanted to do a sweet one for a child's (or adult's) birthday, blackberry and apple would be good. You could even add cocoa powder to the sweet pastry to make it darker and serve it with chocolate sauce. I'm sure the Emperor would approve.

Other shapes include Buzz Lightyear, cars, wine bottles, football shirts and shapes such as stars and hearts. Use your imagination. But remember, you don't want a tin too high or complex in shape – this is a pie, not a cake, remember.

The fork is strong in this one'
The trick is to make the pie, cook it, cool, and then turn it out on to the plate. You'll need to blind bake the face side until almost cooked through. Baking beads are critical, otherwise the pastry will contract and rise out of the dips and features of the tin, and will lose definition. A thicker than normal layer of pastry will help maintain structural integrity too. Finally I'd recommend having a test run to make sure things work – you don't want someone's big day ruined by a badly turned out pie. If your test pie works, you can pop it in the freezer and enjoy it another time

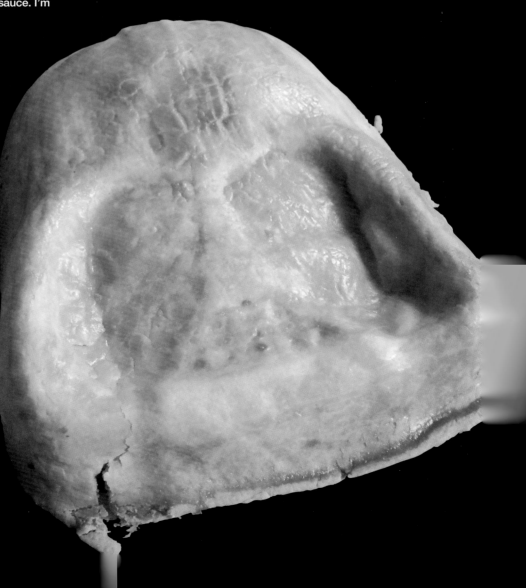

THE BRITISH PIE AWARDS

The town of Melton Mowbray can be said to be the spiritual home of British pies, lending its name to one of our finest examples of the art of pie-making – the Melton Mowbray pork pie. Indeed, the 'MMPP' was the first of the UK's regional pies to be awarded a PGI statute by the EU. It's fitting, then, that the annual British Pie Awards takes place in the town's parish church.

Nearly 1,000 pies from small independent butchers to large-scale producers come from all over the UK to compete in a range of categories, with one perfect pie being crowned the Champion of Champions.

The judging takes place on or around

St George's Day, and is a sight to behold. The church is bedecked with bunting, and filled with the warming smells of pies being heated and sent to the teams of judges. The logistics of keeping track of over 1,000 pies is mind blowing, yet each is examined for boil out, soggy bottoms, texture, taste and bake quality.

Standing at the altar, looking out over a congregation of a thousand pies, you really get a sense of the huge range of sizes and shapes in this census of British pies. It's also quite clear that we do love pies in this country.

I've had the honour of judging a range of different categories over the years. Now, eating pies for a day sounds like a dream job, and I'll admit it's great fun, but you have to be careful: many a newbie judge has come a cropper and 'hit the wall' midway through judging. Pace, gentlemen, is what's needed here. Pace and small bites.

Afterwards pie-makers, judges and anyone else repairs to the pub next door to wash it all down with a glass or two of beer.

Football pies

'Who ate all the pies?' is a popular football chant aimed at the more portly players, officials and managers of Association Football. Indeed, as the author of this book I've had it levelled at myself many a time too.

Pie is the traditional half-time accompaniment to a game of footie, particularly in the North of England. Alas, in recent years the honest sports fan has been distracted from this filling and warming traditional food by the likes of burgers and hot dogs, whilst at some London Premiership clubs there's even crepes and pad Thai on offer – *shudder*.

However, relegate yourself down to the lower leagues and you can still find pies; and no entry on football pies would be complete without mentioning the mighty Morecambe FC (aka The Shrimps). Morecambe are

blessed in the hospitality department with the talents of Graham Aimson, who makes pies sold at the ground. Some 700 to 1,600 pies are sold at each match, and the current range on offer includes chicken, ham and leek, meat and potato, steak and ale, chilli, and cheese and onion to help fans cheer on The Shrimps.

Sadly for Morecambe FC's owners and players their trophy cabinet doesn't contain much silverware for their efforts on the pitch. What it does contain is trophies for Graham's pastry efforts. He won Champion of Champions at the 2011 British Pie Awards, as well as best football pie.

Piebury Corner, based in Arsenal's home patch of Highbury, is another pie-maker producing great football pies. Here each pie is named after one of the Gunners' famous players, so the Ian Wright pie features lamb, veg and a hint of mint, while the Thierry Henry offers venison and red wine gravy, and the late legendary odd-job and groundsman Paddy Galligan is immortalised in pie form with a filling of beef with Guinness.

There's something proper about a pie and a pint at the footie, don't you think? Well, one club owner that doesn't think so is Dale Vince, chairman of Forest Green Rovers FC (based in Nailsworth, Gloucestershire). In 2011 Vince, who is a vegan, took the step of removing red meat from the food on offer at the ground and replacing traditional offerings with either vegetable or sustainably farmed or caught chicken and fish. So instead fans are offered veggie burgers, harvester tuna salad baps and winter root power salads. This has, amazingly, led to an increase in attendance...

APPENDICES

Troubleshooting

It happens to every cook, even the professionals, believe me. Sometimes things don't turn out quite as planned; an eye off the ball here, a dash of complacency there. Normally there's a good reason why things have gone wrong. Sometimes it feels like it's simply the wrath of the gods. When cooking anything, including pies, there's always the potential for something to go wrong. I've had some great disasters in the kitchen; I mistook a jar of tomato purée for pesto, I forgot to add the sugar to custard, I've burnt things – including myself – many times. I once made a braised rabbit dish that was like an old shoe floating in cider. The best thing you can do is not get stressed, know your equipment and recipe, and plan ahead. Allow time for errors, for fixing things, and for a back-up plan. If things don't work out, always have plenty of booze and snacks handy, and some cheese. That'll keep people going. Failing that, send out for pizza.

HELP! I'VE NOT ENOUGH PASTRY OR FILLING!

When this happens you need to consider what to do next.

Option 1. Use a smaller tin. This will increase your pie-to-tin ratio. If you've put the pastry in the tin, added the filling and don't have enough for the lid, spoon out the filling into a bowl and gently remove the pastry by sliding it into a smaller tin. Don't try to pick up the pastry and filling: it'll tear, your filling will fall through and your pastry will be ruined.

Option 2. Make more pastry. Put the half-made pie in the fridge, break out the butter and flour and rustle up another batch of pastry for the lid. It won't take that long. Alternatively, always have a packet of pre-made pastry on standby. A quick defrost in the microwave and it's ready to rock.

Option 3. Not enough filling. It happens. What looks like a huge saucepan brimming with raw ingredients cooks down slowly for hours into something half that size. It's easy to misjudge. If your pie filling is a long, slow-cooked one, it's very hard to somehow bulk it out. I'd try option 1. If, however, it's one of the chicken recipes, you can bulk it out by adding a tin of pulses – something like cannellini beans would be good. The king of bulk, however, is potato. Peel two, dice small, and cook in boiling water before draining, and in 20 minutes you can easily add a third more mass to your filling. Rice, pasta and other carbs will also work.

HOW TO AVOID A SOGGY BOTTOM

The dreaded soggy bottom is something all pie makers come across every now and then. First let's look at how it's got to this stage, then at possible ways to fix it.

Soggy bottoms happen for two reasons: either there isn't enough heat underneath your pie in the oven to cook the pastry, or your filling is too wet and has seeped into your dough. If you're lucky you can see where this has happened, as your pastry may look a little discoloured by the filling.

If your oven has an element at the bottom as well as the top you could try putting the pie back in the tin and finish cooking like that. (On some ovens this function is called 'pizza mode').

If you've not got this option, another way to save your pie is to place it back in its tin, and into a flat-bottomed frying pan on a very low heat. This should help transfer some heat to the pastry and cook it. But be warned you're very much on a wing and a prayer here.

Sadly one only finds out about a soggy bottom when you're dishing up. Which is why you should always make pies slightly in advance, check they're OK, and if so leave them somewhere warm while you get on with the accompaniments.

Prevention is better than cure, however, so to avoid a soggy bottom from the outset try blind baking the pie case first. Another tip is to give the part-baked pastry casts a brush with beaten egg on the inside and pop in your hot oven for a few moments more until the egg is cooked. This then forms a barrier between the filling and the pastry, which should help lessen any seepage. Finally, always use a slotted spoon to transfer your filling to the pie case. That way you can put in the 'bits' first, then top up with the sauce, further reducing or thickening with cornflour if needed.

Another cause of SB is that your pastry is too thick at the bottom – thick pastry takes longer to cook. In most cases you should aim for the thickness of a pound coin.

'It's not good, I can't save it'

Well, perhaps it's best to chalk this up to experience. As long as your pastry isn't actually raw, I think most dinner guests can forgive a slightly soggy bottom in places. Alternatively take a knife and scalp the top half of the pie. Pour the warm filling into another pie dish and place the top on, thus turning a double-cruster into a single-crust pie. Place the soggy bottom half back in the oven and cook it anyway.

OTHER PASTRY ERRORS

My pastry won't stay together

Sometimes pastry can feel less like a sheet of flexible golden dough and more like a pile of wet sand. If this happens, just try working it a little more to develop the gluten in the flour. This will help keep your pastry together.

Boil over

Boil over or boil out occurs when your filling expands during cooking and pushes out through the lid and the bottom of the pie. A little boil out is OK – it caramelises and adds an umami note to your pie. Too much is a bad thing, though, as your pie will lose structure. Don't overload your pies with filling: you just want it snug. Also try turning the heat down a little if you spot boil out.

My puff pastry isn't puffed up!

This can happen. Puff pastry needs to go from very cold to very hot very quickly. That way the water in the butter turns to steam quickly, and expands the space between. The fat melts and cooks the dough. Consequently you need to get your oven very hot, 200°C minimum. Never leave puff pastry sitting about at room temperature. Take if from the fridge at the last minute, work it into shape, then chill it again if it's become too warm.

Liquid is the enemy of puff pastry too. If it touches your filling for too long it'll get soggy and never puff up. This can result in a soggy middle of a puff-topped pie. If this happens, invest in a pie bird. They help keep the middle up and off the filling. Also, make sure your filling is cold when it goes in the oven.

Rescuing a pie in this condition is tricky, your options being to either remove the lid and transfer to a hot baking tray or to switch on the grill to get some direct heat at the middle. It's why I think puff is more of a pain than shortcrust when it comes to savoury pies.

Suppliers

Lakeland.co.uk

This Cumbrian-based firm prides itself on its customer service and attention to detail. If you buy one of their own-branded products it comes with a lifetime guarantee – even if the receipt has long since turned to dust. Consequently they've been trusted by housewives, cooks and chefs for ages.

For many years they operated via mail order, but they've now also branched out into shops in major shopping areas, meaning you can examine and try a range of different products in store as well as have a chat with their knowledgeable staff.

Their bakeware is excellent (it's what I use) and will last you forever. They even have an electric pie maker, which turns out perfect pies every time, and in under ten minutes.

delicious. magazine

Every recipe in delicious. is tested and checked in the magazine's studio kitchen to make sure it not only works, but that it tastes amazing too. Go on, treat yourself with a subscription.

pierate.co.uk

Reviews for pretty much every kind of commercially available pie you can get in the UK. Each pie is scored using the Seven Cs: colour, consistency, capacity, chewiness, cheapness, content and condition.

britishpieawards.co.uk

All the information on the annual British Pie Awards, should you want to enter one of your creations.

pieburycorner.com

Situated near the Arsenal football ground. A Piebury Corner pie is a much needed staple for many a Gooner.

helengraves.co.uk

One of my favourite writers, Helen's food is as amazing as her writing is funny.

Gingerpig.co.uk

Fab meat from Yorkshire available in central London. Look out for their 100-day-old cockerels around Christmas time – they're massive and have a rich, complex flavour.

perfectpie.co.uk

Lovely pies from North Norfolk.

INDEX